## Opening up
# Ezra

**PETER WILLIAMS**

DayOne

Opening up
Ezra

PETER WILLIAMS

Ezra the scribe was the instrument for the reformation that took place when the people of God began to return to the Promised Land. We are told that he 'prepared his heart to seek the Law of the LORD, and to do it, and to teach statutes and ordinances in Israel' (Ezra 7:10). He is a man for our time, setting us a great example in his tireless efforts to bring his people back to God's Word.

Peter Williams' skilful exposition of this neglected book equips the reader with helpful background information and applies the message of the book of Ezra to individual Christians and to the Church in the twenty-first century. I am confident that it will be become a valuable tool for personal and group study, and my prayer is that God will use the message of this exposition to raise up people like Ezra in our day.

Simon J Robinson,
Author and senior pastor of Walton Evangelical Church,
Chesterfield, England

© Day One Publications 2006
First printed 2006

ISBN 1 84625 022 -6

9 781846 250224

British Library Cataloguing in Publication Data available

Published by Day One Publications
Ryelands Road, Leominster, HR6 8NZ
Telephone 01568 613 740   FAX 01568 611 473

email—sales@dayone.co.uk
web site—www.dayone.co.uk
North American—e-mail-sales@dayonebookstore.com
North American web site—www.dayonebookstore.com

Designed by Steve Devane and printed by Gutenberg Press, Malta

*Dedicated to
Alec,
a faithful brother in the Lord*

# List of Bible abbreviations

| THE OLD TESTAMENT | | 1 Chr. | 1 Chronicles | Dan. | Daniel |
|---|---|---|---|---|---|
| | | 2 Chr. | 2 Chronicles | Hosea | Hosea |
| Gen. | Genesis | Ezra | Ezra | Joel | Joel |
| Exod. | Exodus | Neh. | Nehemiah | Amos | Amos |
| Lev. | Leviticus | Esth. | Esther | Obad. | Obadiah |
| Num. | Numbers | Job | Job | Jonah | Jonah |
| Deut. | Deuteronomy | Ps. | Psalms | Micah | Micah |
| Josh. | Joshua | Prov. | Proverbs | Nahum | Nahum |
| Judg. | Judges | Eccles. | Ecclesiastes | Hab. | Habakkuk |
| Ruth | Ruth | S.of.S. | Song of Solomon | Zeph. | Zephaniah |
| 1 Sam. | 1 Samuel | Isa. | Isaiah | Hag. | Haggai |
| 2 Sam. | 2 Samuel | Jer. | Jeremiah | Zech. | Zechariah |
| 1 Kings | 1 Kings | Lam. | Lamentations | Mal. | Malachi |
| 2 Kings | 2 Kings | Ezek. | Ezekiel | | |

| THE NEW TESTAMENT | | Gal. | Galatians | Heb. | Hebrews |
|---|---|---|---|---|---|
| | | Eph. | Ephesians | James | James |
| Matt. | Matthew | Phil. | Philippians | 1 Peter | 1 Peter |
| Mark | Mark | Col. | Colossians | 2 Peter | 2 Peter |
| Luke | Luke | 1 Thes. | 1 Thessalonians | 1 John | 1 John |
| John | John | 2 Thes. | 2 Thessalonians | 2 John | 2 John |
| Acts | Acts | 1 Tim. | 1 Timothy | 3 John | 3 John |
| Rom. | Romans | 2 Tim. | 2 Timothy | Jude | Jude |
| 1 Cor. | 1 Corinthians | Titus | Titus | Rev. | Revelation |
| 2 Cor. | 2 Corinthians | Philem. | Philemon | | |

# Overview

After the Southern Kingdom of Israel, Judah, had been taken into captivity in Babylon, and had stayed there for seventy years—a time known as the Exile—the time came for the Jews to return to their own land. Ezra and Nehemiah were key leaders in bringing the people back and helping them to become re-established in their own land.

### Post-exilic books of the Old Testament

Ezra, Nehemiah, Esther, Haggai, Zechariah and Malachi are books which all cover the same general period in Bible history, and the same subject matter concerning the return of God's people from exile in Babylon. This means they contain the final section of God's revelation under the old covenant before the coming of Christ in the New Testament.

### The chronology of Ezra and the main characters

**Cyrus the Great**—Conquered the Babylonian empire in 538 B.C. and changed the balance of power in the ancient world in favour of the Persians.

**Zerubbabel**—The leader of the first group of exiles to return home, and the civil governor of Judah under Cyrus, mentioned in Zechariah 4:6-10.

▶ Page 10

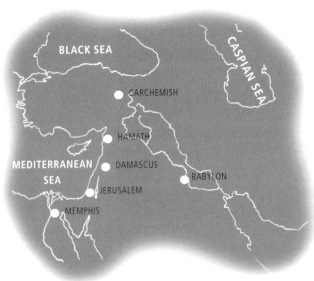

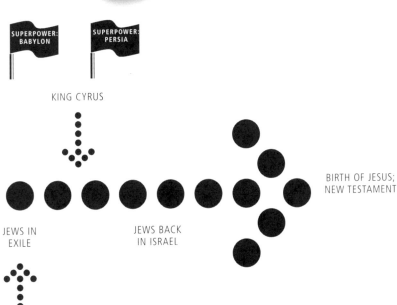

SUPERPOWER: BABYLON

SUPERPOWER: PERSIA

KING CYRUS

JEWS IN EXILE

JEWS BACK IN ISRAEL

BIRTH OF JESUS; NEW TESTAMENT

BABYLONIAN CAPTIVITY

OPENING UP EZRA

◁ **Jeshua, also called Joshua**—The high priest who shared the leadership with Zerubbabel. Mentioned in Zechariah 3:1.

**Darius I**—King of Persia who came to the throne in 522 B.C.—Mentioned in Zechariah 1:1.

The building of the temple in Jerusalem was completed in 515 B.C. during the reign of Darius I.

**Artaxerxes**—King of Persia 464-424 B.C. He gave Ezra permission to return to Jerusalem with the second group of exiles.

Ezra arrived in Jerusalem in 458 B.C.

The map on page 9 shows the probable route of the return of the Jews from Babylon—along the River Euphrates to Carchemish, and then down past Hamath and Damascus to Jerusalem—a journey of approximately 900 miles.

# Background and summary

The book of Ezra is a straightforward account of one of the most important periods in the ancient history of Israel—the return of the Jews to their homeland after seventy years of exile in Babylon. The books of Ezra and Nehemiah overlap to a certain extent, although it is probable that Ezra had arrived in Jerusalem and had completed his work before Nehemiah appeared on the scene. The period covered by the book of Ezra is about ninety-three years—538 B.C. to 445 B.C.

The book divides itself naturally into two parts. Chapters 1-6 record the return of the first group of exiles under Sheshbazzar and Zerubbabel the civil leaders, and Jeshua the high priest, and the rebuilding of the altar and the temple. Ezra writes about this, but was not himself involved in that work since he did not arrive in Jerusalem until after the temple had been built (458 B.C.). The second part of the book, chapters 7-10, is both biographical and historical and deals with the return of the second group of exiles under Ezra's leadership and his reformation of the spiritual life of the nation. During this second period Ezra and Nehemiah may have worked for part of that time together.

## Why were the Jews in exile?

To understand the historical events leading up to the exile of the Jews in Babylon we have to go back to the time of

> The southern kingdom of Judah nevertheless itself continued to worship the pagan gods of the surrounding nations. Finally God's patience was exhausted, and judgement came.

Solomon. At the end of Solomon's reign the Jewish nation was divided into two kingdoms, north and south. The northern kingdom under Jeroboam consisted of ten tribes and was known as Israel. The southern kingdom under Rehoboam was known as Judah and consisted of the tribes of Judah and Benjamin. The kings and people of Israel were to try God's patience by their continuing idolatry and disobedience of his law. God, through his servants and prophets Hosea and Amos, warned them again and again that this would lead to judgement and disaster, and it came finally when Shalmaneser king of Assyria conquered Israel and carried its people into exile in 721 B.C. (2 Kings 17:1-6).

The southern kingdom of Judah, in spite of witnessing the tragic downfall of Israel and the warnings given by the prophets Isaiah and Jeremiah, nevertheless itself continued to worship the pagan gods of the surrounding nations. Finally God's patience was exhausted, and judgement came when Nebuchadnezzar, the king of mighty Babylon, invaded Judah in 586 B.C., destroyed the city and the temple, and carried the people into exile. They were to remain in exile in Babylon for seventy years, as prophesied by Jeremiah: 'Therefore thus says the Lord of hosts: "Because you have not heard my words, behold, I will send and take all the families of the north," says the LORD, "and Nebuchadnezzar the king of Babylon, my servant, and will bring them against this land… And this whole land shall be a desolation and an astonishment, and these nations shall serve the king of Babylon seventy years" ' (Jer. 25:8-11).

## Who was Ezra?

All that we know about Ezra is contained in his own book and in Nehemiah. He came from a distinguished priestly family, which traced its history from Aaron, the first high priest of Israel. He was also a scribe, and a diligent student and interpreter of God's law. His desire above all else was to teach the Word of God, and to establish the authority of the Law of Moses in the civil and religious life of the nation (7:1-10).

Ezra was held in high regard by the Persian king of the time, Artaxerxes I, under whom he held an official position as governor of Jerusalem with authority to appoint magistrates and judges, and to administer justice (7:25). As to his character Ezra was deeply devout, a man of prayer, and very sensitive to God's leading in his life. Several times he speaks of the 'good hand' of God being upon him and his companions (7:28; 8:18, 22).

Among Bible scholars there is a strong opinion that Ezra, as a scribe, is not only the author of the book named after him, but also of 1 and 2 Chronicles and Nehemiah. The books of Chronicles and Ezra share common characteristics such as lists of names and genealogies, and in addition the closing verses of 2 Chronicles, verses 22 and 23, are virtually the same, word for word, as the opening verses of Ezra.

Finally, according to ancient Jewish tradition, Ezra lived to a good old age and died on his way back from Jerusalem to the court of Artaxerxes, and was buried somewhere in the region of the river Tigris.

## Why study Ezra?

There are several good reasons for doing so:

**FIRST**, Ezra and the other historical books of the Bible reveal to us the way in which God is involved in the flow of national and international affairs. He does not stand apart from the destiny of nations, but is sovereign over the unfolding processes of history.

**SECOND**, the book, in common with other parts of the Bible, shows how God at times can use the most unlikely people, such as the pagan king Cyrus, to be his instruments for furthering his purposes in the world.

> The book emphasizes the truth that in every age there is the need for reformation and spiritual renewal in the lives of God's people. That lesson has a particular relevance for the church today.

**THIRD**, the book teaches us the necessity for God to refine and discipline the spiritual character of his people through difficult experiences like the exile.

**FOURTH**, one of the most comforting and encouraging truths in this book is the reminder that God is always true to his promises. We shall see that he promised through his servant Jeremiah to bring his people back from exile, and he did exactly that.

**FIFTH**, the book emphasizes the truth that in every age there is the need for reformation and spiritual renewal in the lives of God's people. That lesson has a particular relevance for the church today.

**SIXTH,** in the different roles played by Zerubbabel the governor, Joshua the high priest, and Ezra the scribe, we see that God always has the right man to match the needs of the hour.

History always has a lot to teach us, and that is no less true of the book of Ezra with its many lessons which I hope I have drawn out and applied to Christians in the church today. Among much else that he did, Ezra brought about a spiritual reformation among God's people, and such reformation is something the church needs in every age if it is to remain relevant. Similarly, individual Christians need to assess the quality of their own faith from time to time, and to reform their thinking and behaviour should it become necessary.

# 1 The proclamation of Cyrus

(1:1-11)

The book of Ezra is a powerful and remarkable example of prophecy being converted into history.

This is clear from the opening verses, where Cyrus the king of Persia issues a decree allowing the Jews to return to their homeland.

## The exile comes to an end

Now in the first year of Cyrus king of Persia, that the word of the LORD by the mouth of Jeremiah might be fulfilled, the LORD stirred up the spirit of Cyrus king of Persia, so that he made a proclamation throughout all his kingdom, and also put it in writing, saying, Thus says Cyrus king of Persia: All the kingdoms of the earth the LORD God of heaven has given me. And he has commanded me to build him a house at Jerusalem which is in Judah. Who is among you of all his people? May his God be with him, and let him go up to

Jerusalem, which is in Judah, and build the house of the Lord God of Israel (he is God), which is in Jerusalem' (1:1-3).

Cyrus is described as the 'king of Persia', but at the time of issuing the proclamation he is actually ruling in Babylon where the Jews had been living in exile over a long period. What had happened was this. Cyrus was king of the Medes and Persians but in 538 B.C. he conquered Babylon on the night of Belshazzar's feast, when Daniel had just been made third ruler in the kingdom. 'That very night Belshazzar, king of the Chaldeans, was slain. And Darius the Mede received the kingdom, being about sixty-two years old' (Dan. 5:30-31). Darius the Mede and Cyrus king of Persia are considered by some to be one and the same person.

Jeremiah is mentioned in connection with the proclamation because more than seventy years earlier he had prophesied the length of time the Jews would spend in exile in Babylon, and their eventual return home. 'For thus says the Lord: After seventy years are completed at Babylon, I will visit you and perform my good word toward you, and cause you to return to this place' (Jer. 29:10).

An even more amazing prophecy is that of Isaiah who, one hundred and fifty years earlier, actually named Cyrus as the instrument God would use to bring about the restoration of his people: 'Who says of Cyrus, "He is my shepherd, and he shall perform all my pleasure, saying to Jerusalem, 'You shall be built,' and to the temple, 'Your foundation shall be laid' " ' (Isa. 44:28).

## God's faithfulness

The most important lesson to come out of these opening verses is the sheer faithfulness of God in keeping his promises. We have seen that, years earlier in the predictive prophecies of Isaiah and Jeremiah, God had promised to bring his people back to their homeland, and that the temple would be rebuilt. All that was now about to be fulfilled in the proclamation of Cyrus. During the long night of exile God's people must have wondered at times if they would ever see Jerusalem again. We have only to recall the lament of the captives as expressed in Psalm 137:

> By the rivers of Babylon,
> There we sat down, yea, we wept
> When we remembered Zion.
> We hung our harps
> Upon the willows in the midst of it.
> For there those who carried us away captive asked of us a
> , song,
> And those who plundered us requested mirth,
> Saying, 'Sing us one of the songs of Zion!'
> How shall we sing the LORD's song
> In a foreign land?
> (vv. 1-4)

But God was faithful to his promises and did not forget his people. But then he never does forget. I realize it is not easy to believe that when we are going through our own personal kind of exile and the situation seems dark and gloomy. But that is the kind of situation Satan will exploit by whispering in your ear that God *has* forgotten, and he will tempt you to look at your circumstances rather than to God. For the truth is that at such a time, when everything else has failed, the only thing we have left to rely on is the sheer integrity of God and his Word. As Paul rightly reminds us: 'If we are faithless, he remains faithful; he cannot deny himself' (2 Tim. 2:13). Or as the well-known hymn puts it:

> Great is Thy faithfulness, O God my Father,
>
> there is no shadow of turning with Thee;
>
> Thou changest not, Thy compassions they fail not;
>
> As Thou hast been Thou for ever wilt be.[1]

## God's sovereignty

What strikes us forcefully in this proclamation is the strange and wonderful way in which God uses a pagan king like Cyrus to fulfil his purpose for the restoration of his people. He moved him so '… that he made a proclamation' (1:1). Here we see the sovereign hand of God working through the processes of history. For God created this world and he is concerned with what happens in it and to it. He does not stand apart from the clash of national and international affairs and the rise and fall of nations, but in his sovereign power overrules all things, and directs the events of this world according to his purpose. It is not rulers and governments who have the last word in human affairs. Psalm 2 is a good illustration of that:

> Why do the nations rage,
>
> And the people plot a vain thing?
>
> The kings of the earth set themselves,
>
> And the rulers take counsel together,
>
> Against the LORD and against his Anointed, saying,

'Let us break their bonds in pieces
And cast away their cords from us.'
He who sits in the heavens shall laugh;
The LORD shall hold them in derision.
Then he shall speak to them in his wrath,
And distress them in his deep displeasure;
'Yet I have set my King
On my holy hill of Zion'
(vv. 1-6).

Cyrus himself need not have known that it was God who 'stirred up' his spirit and directed his thoughts to the restoration of his people. On the other hand it might well have been that God used his servant Daniel, who was still in the king's service (Dan. 1:21) to influence Cyrus, and even to inform him of Jeremiah's prophecy which he knew about (Dan. 9:1-2). Either way, it was the sovereign God who was directing events, and that teaches us as Christians to view what is happening on the international scene from the divine perspective. As we watch the news programmes on TV, and see the world scene with its rebelliousness and political unrest and shaky foundations, we might become fearful for the future. But in it all, the judgements and purposes of God are being worked out so that even 'the wrath of man shall praise [him]' (Ps. 76:10).

## God moves the spirit

When the king's decree was made known, what was the response of the people? Not all responded in a positive spirit. We read: 'Then the heads of the fathers' houses of Judah and Benjamin, and the priests and the Levites, with all whose spirits God had moved, arose to go up and build the house of the Lord which is in Jerusalem' (1:5).

Notice the phrase, 'all whose spirits God had moved'. That implies that not everyone among the exiles was moved in their hearts to take advantage of the royal proclamation. And we shall see in the next chapter that there were reasons for that. For the moment we need only emphasize that, in the work of God's kingdom, it is always God himself who takes the initiative in moving people in their spirits to take the direction he plans for them. Those Jews who responded positively did so in spite of the fact that returning home would involve considerable sacrifice and hardship. They were not going on a holiday, but were faced with a hazardous journey of some 900 miles, and the land waiting for them had been devastated, with many of its towns and villages destroyed and its temple razed to the ground. We are inclined to feel, therefore, that if God himself had not moved their spirits, they would not have moved at all!

> When people commit their lives to Christ in a meaningful and lasting way, it is not because they have made a mental decision to do so, but because God himself, by his Holy Spirit, has moved them in their spirits to respond to the message of salvation.

The same principle applies in the experience of Christian conversion. When people commit their lives to Christ in a meaningful and lasting way, it is not because they have made a mental decision to do so, but because God himself, by his Holy Spirit, has moved them in their spirits to respond to the message of salvation. We have a good illustration of this in the conversion of Lydia in Acts: 'Now a certain woman named Lydia heard us. She was a seller of purple from the city of Thyatira, who worshipped God. The Lord opened her heart to heed the things spoken by Paul' (Acts 16:14).

> One of the great names for God in the Bible is Jehovah Jireh (The LORD will provide—Gen. 22:14).

And the converse is equally true: when people make a profession of faith and then quickly fall away, it is because they were only moved at the level of the mind and emotions, but not in the depths of their own spirit by the Spirit of God. Again we have a clear example of this with the confession and baptism of Simon the sorcerer, who tried to purchase with money the power of the Holy Spirit, and Peter said to him: 'You have neither part nor portion in this matter, for your heart is not right in the sight of God. Repent therefore of this your wickedness, and pray God if perhaps the thought of your heart may be forgiven you' (Acts 8:21-22).

## God the provider

One other important lesson to come out of this first chapter is the provision God made for the return of his people. God not only delivered his people from Babylon, but he also provided all the costs for the journey and for the settlement in Jerusalem as well.

In his proclamation Cyrus gave the following instruction: 'And whoever is left in any place where he dwells, let the men of his place help him with silver and gold, with goods and livestock, besides the freewill offerings for the house of God which is in Jerusalem' (1:4). It reminds us of a similar provision God made for the deliverance of his people from slavery in Egypt at the time of the Exodus: 'Now the children of Israel had done according to the word of Moses, and they had asked from the Egyptians articles of silver, articles of gold, and clothing. And the LORD had given the people favour in the sight of the Egyptians, so that they granted them what they requested' (Exod. 12:35-36).

And the provision went even further. Cyrus returned all the sacred vessels Nebuchadnezzar had taken from the temple at the conquest of Jerusalem. 'All the articles of gold and silver were five thousand four hundred. All these Sheshbazzar took with the captives who were brought from Babylon to Jerusalem' (1:11).

One of the great names for God in the Bible is Jehovah Jireh (The LORD will provide—Gen. 22:14). We can apply this truth in three ways.

**FIRST,** there is God's providential care for the world he has created. Many are content to believe that our world, and the whole universe, is the result of mechanical impersonal forces, but the Christian cannot square such an explanation of origins with the revelation given in Scripture. We believe that God brought this world into being and that he cares for it, and provides through the intricate processes and complex structures of nature all that is required for the sustenance of life. As the psalmist puts it:

The eyes of all look expectantly to you,
And you give them their food in due season.
You open your hand
And satisfy the desire of every living thing
(Ps. 145:15-16).

**SECOND,** when God calls a person to a special task he always provides what is necessary for the carrying-out of that task, whether in manpower, money or materials. We could illustrate this in countless ways. Take the case of Hudson Taylor walking on Brighton beach on 25 June 1865. He came to the decision to begin a mission work in central China and wrote in his Bible: 'prayed for twenty-four willing skilful labourers'. Two days later, in faith, he opened an account in the name of the China Inland Mission with the magnificent sum of ten pounds! In the years that followed God provided all that was needed so that it became one of the great faith missions of the Christian world, with hundreds of workers in the field.

Or take the faith work of George Müller of Bristol. On the night he had made known his intention at a public meeting to start an orphanage, he made it clear that no one would ever be asked for money or materials; there would be no charge for admission and no restriction on entry because of class or creed. All those employed as masters, matrons and assistants would be unpaid and had to be believers. At the end of the meeting no collection was made but a lady gave him ten shillings and volunteered for the work. The next day, a husband and wife volunteered their help and also promised to give all their furniture for use in the orphanage. From that point on Müller never looked back, and never lacked support for the work.

**THIRD,** and most wonderful of all, God provided a saviour in the gift of his own Son, the Lord Jesus Christ. As Paul expresses it: 'He who did not spare his own Son, but delivered him up for us all, how shall he not with him also freely give us all things?' (Rom. 8:32). Man cannot provide his own salvation, only God can do that. In the cross of Jesus, life is provided in place of eternal damnation. And in addition to delivering up his Son, God will also freely provide us with 'all things'—the grace needed for each day, the strength to overcome our weakness, and the power to overcome temptation.

> When God calls a person to a special task he always provides what is necessary for the carrying-out of that task, whether in manpower, money or materials.

For further study ▶

1. Look up the prophecy in Isaiah 7:14, and read its fulfilment in Matthew 1:23. What other examples in the Bible can you think of where prophecy is converted into history?

2. The first temple was destroyed by Nebuchadnezzar in 586 B.C. Jesus foretold the destruction of the second temple in A.D. 70. Read Matthew 24, Mark 13, Luke 19:41-44 and 24; why was this temple destroyed?

1. In what ways do we see God's sovereignty at work today?

2. Can you think of other strange instruments in the Bible, like Cyrus, that God used for his purposes?

3. Why was it so important to bring back the articles of temple worship? Do such externals matter in worship today?

4. Does God still provide for his people? Suggest several ways in which this may be seen.

# 2 Going home

(2:1-70)

On the face of it, it might seem hard to find immediate benefit from this chapter, and yet there is much in it that is instructive and helpful!

Ezra chapter 2 is made up of a list of the names of those exiles who were the first to return from Babylon under the leadership of Zerubbabel, the secular governor, and Jeshua, the high priest, in 538 B.C.

'Now these are the people of the province who came back from the captivity, of those who had been carried away, whom Nebuchadnezzar the king of Babylon had carried away to Babylon, and who returned to Jerusalem and Judah, everyone to his own city. Those who came with Zerubbabel were Jeshua, Nehemiah, Seraiah, Reelaiah, Mordecai, Bilshan, Mispar, Bigvai, Rehum, and Baanah'

(2:1-2).

There then follows the list of names.

Before we go any further we must clear up a possible misunderstanding by explaining that Sheshbazzar (1:11) and

Zerubbabel were possibly one and the same person; *Sheshbazzar* might have been the Chaldean or Babylonian form of the Hebrew *Zerubbabel*. This identification carries further weight when we compare Ezra 3:8 with Ezra 5:16, when both names are mentioned in connection with the laying of the foundation of the temple.

## Names and genealogies

To come back to Ezra's list of names: many such lists and genealogies are to be found scattered throughout the Bible, including 1 Chronicles which opens with the genealogy that covers the first nine chapters! But such lists have a sacred purpose, for the history of the Bible is redemptive history, and such lists are meant to show us that God has preserved the chosen people and the promised line of Messiah from generation to generation. Ezra's list of families and tribes tells us two things.

**FIRST,** it was an act of faith; since it expresses the belief of the Jews that the prophecy of return given by Jeremiah would one day be fulfilled, for the record of their families would enable them to claim their ancestral inheritance when back in Judah. To own one's land was very important since it was part of the tribal inheritance, and because, ultimately, the land belonged to the covenant God of Israel. For that reason a person's land could not be sold to a stranger but only to a family or clan member. That was why Naboth would not sell his vineyard to King Ahab (1 Kings 21:3).

In Jeremiah chapter 32 we have another example of faith connected with the ownership of land. When Nebuchadnezzar was besieging Jerusalem, God told

Jeremiah to buy a field from his cousin Hanamel and to keep the deeds 'in an earthen vessel, that they may last many days. For thus says the Lord of hosts, the God of Israel: "Houses and fields and vineyards shall be possessed again in this land"' (v. 14). Here was an act of faith similar to that of the exiles in keeping the record of their families in readiness to claim their inheritance in Judah.

**SECOND,** another reason for keeping a record of families and tribes was to provide proof that those returning were in fact the descendants of the original Jews who had gone into exile. There were some who had not kept their family records (2:59), and among them were some of the priests, who were then excluded from the priesthood (2:62). This generation-to-generation linkage, therefore, was important in identifying the Jews as God's special people, and particularly important in regard to the Messiahship of Jesus, as the genealogies of Matthew and Luke make clear.

## Why so few?

One very significant feature in connection with the list of names is that the total number amounted to fewer than 50,000. 'The whole assembly together was forty-two thousand three hundred and sixty, besides their male and female servants, of whom there were seven thousand three hundred and thirty-seven; and they had two hundred men and women singers' (2:64-65). This was a tiny number in comparison with those who had originally been taken captive. And the question we naturally ask is: why so few?

The explanation may be found in the situation pertaining today. In 1948, the modern state of Israel was established and

Jews began to return to Palestine from all those parts of the world where they had been scattered for nearly two thousand years. But even so, the population of modern Israel is only about four million, whereas the number of Jews living in other countries is about seventeen million. Why this reluctance to return to their homeland? Clearly it is because those Jews living in the USA, the UK, France and elsewhere have become so accustomed to a comfortable and settled form of existence in these countries that they have no wish to exchange it for the hardships and dangers of modern war-torn Israel.

The same explanation applied in Ezra's day. Many of the exiles in Babylon, after the first shock of deportation had passed, had settled down to their change of circumstances and had created a new lifestyle for themselves. Many had become prosperous over the years and had become assimilated into Persian society. Indeed Jeremiah the prophet had urged them, in a letter he wrote, to make the best of their captivity:

> Thus says the LORD of hosts, the God of Israel, to all who were carried away captive…: Build houses and dwell in them; plant gardens and eat their fruit. Take wives and beget sons and daughters; and take wives for your sons and give your daughters to husbands, so that they may bear sons and daughters—that you may be increased there, and not diminished. And seek the peace of the city where I have caused you to be carried away captive, and pray to the LORD for it; for in its peace you will have peace
> (Jer. 29:4-7).

The result was that many of the Jews had become so

comfortable and prosperous that, when the call came for them to return and undertake a journey of some 900 miles to a city in ruins and a temple that no longer existed, they simply could not rise to it. The cost was too great and the shock to their system too disturbing. Dare we criticize them for that? And yet we cannot overlook the fact that they were refusing to live up to their destiny as God's chosen people.

## The demands of faith

Is there a lesson for us here in the church today as God's people? Are we too comfortable in our faith, enjoying a laid-back kind of Christianity? Does the gospel of the Lord Jesus make any real demands upon us involving personal cost and sacrifice? Does it even make demands when it comes to giving of our time, our energy and money in the Lord's work? And what of that other kind of cost in terms of prayer for the ministry of the word, and for the souls of those in the community around, which creates in us a deep 'sighing for God'? How much of that do we see in our churches today?

The truth is that nothing of real and lasting worth is accomplished for God without this willingness for some personal cost and disturbance. And when we reflect upon it, we are bound to confess that no cost we may pay is too much in return for what it cost God to provide our salvation in the death of Christ, and for all he will yet give us in eternity.

## The remnant

There is however a more positive way of considering this question of the small number who returned from the captivity. They constitute the 'remnant' in every age who are aware of their destiny and rise to the challenges of God's kingdom. This doctrine of the remnant runs all through Scripture, and Ezra himself, in his most moving prayer, refers to God's graciousness in permitting a remnant to return to their homeland: 'And now for a little while grace has been shown from the LORD our God, to leave us a remnant to escape, and to give us a peg in his holy place, that our God may enlighten our eyes and give us a measure of revival in our bondage' (9:8).

This doctrine of the remnant has a twofold application. First, it speaks to us as individuals. In every age, however dark and spiritually barren, God will always have those who have been saved by his grace and who remain faithful to him. We may experience loneliness in being one of God's remnant in the place where we work, or in the home, or the school or college, or even in the church where we worship. Our stand for evangelical truth makes us feel isolated. But we are encouraged when we remind ourselves that God has others who are faithful to him, and they are to be found in shops, offices, factories and academic institutions—a modern-day equivalent of 7,000 who have not bowed the knee to our modern Baals and the false gods of today. These are the remnant who one day will receive the crown of life for their faithfulness.

Second, the doctrine of the remnant speaks to the church today. Speaking of the spiritual life of the nation, Isaiah says that they would have been lost 'unless the LORD of hosts had left to us a very small remnant' (Isa. 1:9). And that is our spiritual position. The spiritual life of our nations would be infinitely worse than it is were it not that there is still a godly remnant in existence. There still are churches where the gospel is faithfully preached, who accept the authority of God's Word, who are zealous in evangelizing and reaching out to the community. And whatever spiritual blessing or revival God may again bring to our nations it will be through such churches, and not through those institutional churches and denominations with their ecumenical structures and liberal teaching. It will be through pastors and people who are true to the faith given once for all to the saints, and who make up the faithful remnant of today.

## The arrival home

We are told nothing whatever of the actual journey made by the returning exiles, but in the closing verses of this chapter we are left in no doubt as to what they did on their arrival in Jerusalem. The first thing they did was to assemble on the site of the ruined temple and make a freewill offering for the building of God's house: 'Some of the heads of the fathers' houses, when they came to the house of the LORD which is in Jerusalem, offered freely for the house of God, to erect it in its place. According to their ability, they gave to the treasury for the work sixty-one thousand gold drachmas, five thousand minas of silver, and one hundred priestly garments' (2:68-69).

In making the freewill offering a priority over everything else they were showing that the support and upkeep of God's house was a most serious matter. It is for pastors and church leaders to make it clear to the people that giving to the Lord's work is not a fringe activity but a spiritual obligation. There is a great deal written in Scripture about the whole question of giving to God's work. Here are just three reasons showing the necessity for taking this matter seriously:

**FIRST,** what we give is a token only of our deep gratitude to God for all that he has given us in the gift of salvation through Christ his Son. As Paul puts it, 'Thanks be to God for his indescribable gift!' (2 Cor. 9:15). We can never hope to repay that, but our willingness to give is a token of our love.

**SECOND,** if we acknowledge Christ as Lord, then his lordship and authority extend to every part of our lives, including our giving. What we give to the Lord's treasury therefore cannot be treated as a casual matter, but is obligatory, and part of our recognition of the lordship of Christ in our lives.

**THIRD,** giving generously to God's work brings blessing upon a church and its people, and promotes spiritual growth. To quote Paul again: 'But this I say: He who sows sparingly will also reap sparingly, and he who sows bountifully will also reap bountifully' (2 Cor. 9:6).

There are two other things to be said in connection with the exiles' giving to God's work.

**FIRST,** it was a 'freewill' offering. It had nothing to do with tithing, which is something dealt with separately in Scripture. The freewill offering is something over and above the tithe. I remember reading somewhere, 'God demands our tithes but he deserves our offerings.'

**SECONDLY,** we read here is that the people gave 'according to their ability' (2:69). God measures smallness and largeness by a totally different standard from us. That is why Jesus said of the widow's offering: '[She] has put in more than all those who have given to the treasury; for they all put in out of their abundance, but she out of her poverty' (Mark 12:43-44). Men will ask, how *much* do we give? God asks, *how* do we give? It is not the gift that is paramount with God, but the spirit of the giver.

## The right priorities

The other thing the exiles did on their return was to disperse to their own towns and villages and start rebuilding their homes and their lives. But that was only after they had made provision for the building of the temple. So they had the right order of priorities. God's work came first, and only then did they give their attention to their own personal concerns. That is not always the case with Christians.

For too many it is the other way about. God has a place in their lives, but it is not always the first place; other things, such as their families, homes, careers, or pleasures, are given greater priority and God has to compete with these things for the central place. And that is not how it should be, for God has made it perfectly clear in his word that he is a 'jealous God' (Exod. 20:5) and will not come second to any one or any thing. And as long as we downgrade him in our lives, so long will the quality of our discipleship be of a secondary nature and we shall never fulfil our true potential as his children.

Moreover, as the apostle makes clear, we are all, as Christians, going to be judged one day on the quality of our discipleship here below. 'For we must all appear before the judgement seat of Christ, that each one may receive the things done in the body, according to what he has done, whether good or bad' (2 Cor. 5:10).

**FOR FURTHER STUDY**

1. Read through the genealogies of Jesus in Matthew 1:1-17 and Luke 3:23-38; how do they differ, and why? The genealogy in Ruth 4:18-22 will help.

2. God did not want his people to become absorbed into the Babylonian culture so he brought them back to Jerusalem. Read Daniel 1; how did Daniel resist that kind of assimilation?

**TO THINK ABOUT AND DISCUSS**

1. Compared with Christians in poorer countries, are we in the West too comfortable in our lifestyle to meet the challenges of today?

2. What is the role of the 'remnant' in today's society?

3. What place does tithing have in today's church? Has it been superseded by the principle of the freewill offering?

4. How is a Christian to determine his or her order of priorities?

# 3 A time to build

(3:1-13)

Chapter 2 ended with the exiles making provision for the building of God's house, and then dispersing to their respective towns and villages to commence the work of rebuilding their own homes. But scarcely had they begun providing for their families when the call came from the leaders for them to return to Jerusalem to begin the work on building the altar and the temple.

## As one man

And when the seventh month had come, and the children of Israel were in the cities, the people gathered together as one man to Jerusalem' (3:1). The phrase 'gathered together as one man' clearly speaks of unity of purpose. The seventh month, Tishri in the Jewish calendar, corresponded to our October and had a particularly sacred character for the Jewish people since it was the season of three great religious festivals—the Feast of Trumpets, the Day of Atonement and the Feast of Tabernacles. It was a particularly appropriate time therefore for the people to revive the nation's religious life by starting work on the altar and the temple. They were evidently united and zealous in this desire to re-establish the old ways of truth and righteousness, for they were quite prepared to leave their fields, and the rebuilding of their own homes, in order to gather as 'one man' in Jerusalem for the work of reconstruction.

When a local church or company of Christian people is united as 'one man' with the same purpose, desiring to promote the gospel of Christ, the possibilities are incalculable. Paul had this kind of unity among believers in mind when he used the same expression as we have here in Ezra to urge the Philippian Christians to 'stand firm in one spirit, contending as *one man* for the faith of the gospel' (Phil. 1:27, NIV).

When Paul talks of 'contending' for the gospel, he is thinking of the warfare Christians are engaged in with the forces of darkness, and which they cannot hope to win unless they are united in Christ. For where there is tension and division in a church, Satan is quick to exploit it, so that Christian witness becomes useless.

From an altogether different perspective, evangelical Christians need to be united in their stand for biblical truth and doctrine in the face of pressures from the ecumenical movement; not that ecumenism is any longer the dynamic force it once claimed to be. But indifference and apathy towards biblical authority and doctrinal issues among liberal church leaders still have to be strongly resisted in the interests of the truth. It goes without saying of course, that when evangelicals speak out against liberal church leaders and their attempts to dilute the gospel, it must always be with courtesy and Christian love.

But what about evangelical believers themselves in their relationships with one another? We have to be honest, and admit that it is not all 'sweetness and light' in some Bible-believing churches. There may be unity 'as one man' in their struggle against the forces of evil in the world, and against any dilution of Bible truth; but among themselves there is always the tendency to fly apart, and thereby minimize the effectiveness of the church's witness.

> As members of God's family we are meant to live in peace and unity with one another, in spite of differences of points of view, or temperament, or anything else

As members of God's family we are meant to live in peace and unity with one another, in spite of differences of points of view, or temperament, or anything else. John says, 'That which we have seen and heard we declare to you, that you also may have fellowship with us; and truly our fellowship is with the Father and with his Son Jesus Christ' (1 John 1:3). He is saying that if we have been brought by grace into fellowship with God in Christ, then that same fellowship must extend to all fellow-believers within the family. Failure to practise that indicates a fundamental weakness in our relationship with God.

## The altar principle

After the people had assembled at Jerusalem, Jeshua and Zerubbabel got the work of re-construction under way.

> Then Jeshua the son of Jozadak and his brethren the priests, and Zerubbabel the son of Shealtiel and his brethren, arose and built the altar of the God of Israel, to offer burnt offerings on it, as it is written in the Law of Moses the man of God. Though fear had come upon them because of the people of those countries, they set the altar on its bases; and they offered burnt offerings on it to the LORD, both the morning and evening burnt offerings (Ezra 3:2-3).

This represented an important first step in the work of revitalizing the nation's religious life, since the altar was the place of sacrifice, repentance, rededication, and acceptance by God. Before the greater work of rebuilding the temple could commence, there was this need felt in the hearts of the people to erect the altar, and to get right with God. This altar principle of cleansing, thanksgiving and renewal occurs again and again in Scripture. Here are some examples.

When Noah came out of the ark after the desolation of the flood, and was faced with the colossal task of reconstruction, the first thing he did was to build an altar. 'Then Noah built an altar to the LORD, and took of every clean animal and of every clean bird, and offered burnt offerings on the altar. And the LORD smelled a soothing aroma. Then the LORD said in his heart, "I will never again curse the ground for man's sake, although the imagination of man's heart is evil from his youth; nor will I again destroy every living thing as I have done" ' (Gen. 8:20-21). Noah was thanking God for his deliverance and the opportunity of a new beginning of life on earth.

When Abram arrived in Canaan, the Promised Land, the first thing he did was to build an altar. 'Then the LORD appeared to Abram and said, "To your descendants I will give this land." And there he built an altar to the LORD, who had appeared to him' (Gen. 12:7). In this, Abram was consecrating himself as the foundation builder of the chosen nation, and he was also sending out a clear message to the pagan Canaanites that he worshipped the true and living God.

When Elijah challenged the false prophets of Baal on Mount Carmel, the first thing he did, prior to his great prayer, was to rebuild the altar. 'Then Elijah said to all the people, "Come near to me." So all the people came near to him. And he repaired the altar of the LORD that was broken down' (1 Kings 18:30). By repairing the altar, Elijah was saying that the people had to get back to a right relationship with God through worship and prayer, if the nation's spiritual life was to be revived, and Baalism defeated.

In the light of these examples we can see why the leaders and the people applied themselves to rebuilding the altar before starting work on the temple. Without the altar as the place of sacrifice and getting right with God, a magnificent temple building would have been meaningless. We have plenty of magnificent church structures in the UK today— cathedrals, abbeys, ancient churches—but the spiritual life of the nation is in a bad way. Millions of pounds are spent on preserving and maintaining these buildings, when a tenth of that effort directed to rebuilding the broken altar of God in people's hearts and lives would be infinitely more profitable for the spiritual and moral well-being of the nation.

The apostle Paul was so right when he warned us in his second letter to Timothy that 'in the last days perilous times will come' (2 Tim. 3:1). We are in such a stressful time now, where the church of God is concerned; for while there is no lack of religion today, it so often takes the form of an external religiosity centred in outward forms and buildings. To quote Paul again from the same passage, the church today is content with 'a form of godliness but denying its power' (2 Tim. 3:5).

One other thing needs to be said about the altar principle, which has a more personal application. In past years it was not uncommon to hear the phrase 'the family altar' used in Christian circles. It meant simply the recognition of the importance of prayer and Bible reading within the home. It is a commonplace to make the point yet again that so much of the antisocial behaviour among young people today can be traced back to the breakdown in home and family life. Only the gospel offers a radical solution to this problem by once again making our homes God-centred.

But even Christian households are failing in this, for family prayer and Bible reading are no longer part of the routine of family life. And it is for Christian husbands and fathers to take the lead. They are the heads of the households, and should initiate a move in this direction in the way Jeshua and Zerubbabel took the lead in rebuilding the altar.

## Then and now

With the altar restored, the people, under their leaders, next reinstituted the traditional forms of worship, which had existed before the exile.

> They also kept the Feast of Tabernacles, as it is written, and offered the daily burnt offerings in the number required by ordinance for each day. Afterwards they offered the regular burnt offering, and those for New Moons and for all the appointed feasts of the LORD that were consecrated, and those of everyone who willingly offered a freewill offering to the LORD. From the first day of the seventh month they began to offer burnt offerings to the LORD, although the foundation of the temple of the LORD had not been laid
> (3:4-6).

There are two comments we would make on this.

**FIRST**, there was a desire among the people and their leaders to establish continuity with their past. The exile in Babylon had been a parenthesis in their history, and now that they were back in their homeland they wanted to pick up the threads of the past, both historically and spiritually, by keeping the Feast of Tabernacles. And that was a good thing. We modern-day Christians can learn from that. It is one reason why I believe the study of church history can be so encouraging and helpful to pastors engaged in preaching and teaching the Word of God.

To begin with, we discover that many of the problems and difficulties confronting us in the church today were present in the days of our forefathers. They felt at times, as we do, that things were 'never as bad as they are now', and yet by the grace of God they came through those times and carried on the work. Such was the experience of men like Augustine, Columba, Bernard of Clairvaux, Luther, Tyndale, Whitefield, Wesley and others. What is more, even when these great men passed on, God's work continued, because others were raised up to take their place. We shall see later that the leaders Jeshua and Zerubbabel passed on, but the work of reconstruction and revival continued under Ezra.

Always we must keep in the forefront of our minds the thought that the work of the kingdom of God is much greater than those who are involved in it. The Lord Jesus said, 'I will build my church, and the gates of Hades shall not prevail against it' (Matt. 16:18). Or, to put it another way: 'God buries his workmen, but he carries on his work.'

**SECOND,** in reconstructing the traditional forms of worship, the Jews were looking back to the *greatness and power of God*. When they celebrated the Feast of Tabernacles, what were they thinking about? We are told what it all meant in the 23rd chapter of Leviticus. It told of the time when God, by his great power, cared for his people during the exodus from Egypt and their wandering in the wilderness for forty years. And as the exiles reflected on that great truth, they would be reminded that they too had just experienced their own exodus from Babylon, and that it was the same mighty God who had cared for them in exile, and on the long journey back to their homeland. They would have been greatly encouraged by that, for they knew that God would continue to do for them what he had done for their fathers.

It may be that some of us today are dominated by the

thought that God was somehow active in the past and did
great things, but that he is not so active now—like the
little girl listening to her granny reading the great stories
of the Bible and saying, 'Wasn't God exciting then,
Granny?'

Are we tempted, admittedly in a day of small things, to
think that God is no longer exciting, and that all his great
deeds are in the past? Nothing is more soul-destroying, or
further from the truth. God is always exciting, and he is
always doing things. The Lord Jesus said: 'My Father has
been working until now, and I have been working' (John
5:17). And he still is working. I know the kind of thing that is
said so often. 'Ah, times have changed. Things are very
different in our gospel-hardened age. The problems facing us
are so complex, and totally unlike anything our forefathers
had to face.' But let us be honest: God has not changed, and
that is all that matters. He is still the 'living' God, and Jesus
Christ is still the 'same yesterday, today and forever' (Heb.
13:8). What he was, he still is; and what he did, he still does.
Let us hold on to that.

## Joy and sadness

With the altar rebuilt, and the traditional forms of worship
restored, the people and their leaders next turned their
attention to the building of the temple.

> Now in the second month of the second year of their coming
> to the house of God at Jerusalem, Zerubbabel the son of
> Shealtiel, Jeshua the son of Jozadak, and the rest of their
> brethren the priests and the Levites, and all those who had
> come out of the captivity to Jerusalem, began work and

appointed the Levites from twenty years old and above to oversee the work of the house of the LORD (3:8).

A day came when the foundation of the temple was complete. It was a historical and colourful occasion with a great deal of ceremony, ritual, music and singing.

When the builders laid the foundation of the temple of the LORD, the priests stood in their apparel with trumpets, and the Levites, the sons of Asaph, with cymbals, to praise the LORD, according to the ordinance of David king of Israel. And they sang responsively, praising and giving thanks to the LORD:

"For he is good,
For his mercy endures forever toward Israel."

Then all the people shouted with a great shout, when they praised the LORD, because the foundation of the house of the LORD was laid'
(3:10-11).

But it was also a deeply moving occasion with a mixture of sadness and joy. 'But many of the priests and Levites and heads of the fathers' houses, old men who had seen the first temple, wept with a loud voice when the foundation of this temple was laid before their eyes. Yet many shouted aloud for joy so that the people could not discern the noise of the shout of joy from the noise of the weeping of the people, for the people shouted with a loud shout, and the sound was heard afar off' (3:12-13).

We can understand why there were shouts of joy, but why were the old men weeping? One reason could be that they were comparing the dimensions of the present temple with the hugeness and magnificence of Solomon's temple of some fifty years earlier, and which they could easily remember. If that was the case, it was wrong thinking. The prophet Haggai seems to confirm this, for some fifteen years later, when the work of building was still under way, he said this to the people: 'Who is left among you who saw this temple in its former glory? And how do you see it now? In comparison with it, is this not in your eyes as nothing?' But then he goes on: ' "The glory of this latter temple shall be greater than the former," says the LORD of hosts. "And in this place I will give peace," says the LORD of hosts' (Hag. 2:3, 9). As we suggested earlier, it is not the external magnificence of our church buildings that is of greatest importance, but what goes on inside them.

But another more positive reason might explain the old men's weeping. They could have been remembering what had made this day of celebration necessary. It was the nation's sin and idolatry, and disobedience to God's law, that had brought divine judgement upon them in the form of the exile in Babylon. They were upset when they called to mind how they and their fathers had grieved God. If that were so, their weeping was not a bad thing, for the tears were those of repentance. It is right that we shed tears at times when we recall how often we grieve the Holy Spirit and wound God's heart by the poor quality of our Christian lives.

## Emotion in worship

What comes through to us in this picture of celebration is the deep and profound emotion of the people expressing itself in shouts of joy and loud weeping. It was, in fact, a very noisy act of worship. 'The people could not discern the noise of the shout of joy from the noise of the weeping of the people, for the people shouted with a loud shout, and the sound was heard afar off' (3:13).

The place of emotion in worship has long been a controversial subject among Christians. On the one hand there have been those who have discouraged any expression of emotion in worship, believing it can be dangerous, since people can get carried away by their feelings with disastrous results. That is undoubtedly true. In 2004 we celebrated the centenary of the last great revival in the UK, the 1904 revival in Wales led by Evan Roberts. It was a time of a great outpouring of the Holy Spirit's power, and over 100,000 people were added to the churches. But there was also a certain amount of emotional extravagance in the meetings, with people shouting, screaming hysterically, falling down, giving out prophecies, and claiming to have visions. Jonathan Edwards experienced similar happenings in his revival meetings during the Evangelical Awakening in New England in the eighteenth century. At the same time, George Whitefield and John Wesley were witnessing the same spiritual phenomena in the Evangelical Revival in the UK. And in our own day we have had a resurgence of this kind of physical excitement in the charismatic movement.

What are we to make of it all? I believe we need to be very discerning, and not too ready to write off all forms of

> The place of emotion in worship has long been a controversial subject among Christians.

emotion in worship as merely hysterical, psychological, or even satanic. After all, we are not made of concrete, and God created us with emotions. Also, we must beware of being so concerned with seemliness and order in worship that it degenerates into a dead formality and cold intellectualism. Let us face it: we have good sound Bible-believing churches where the members of the congregation could not shout 'hallelujah' to save their lives!

In the end, it is all a matter of wisdom, and keeping a balance between the mind and the heart, for the Holy Spirit ministers to both. Something that has helped me to keep the whole question of emotion in worship in perspective is a quotation from C. S. Lewis's *Screwtape Letters*: 'To express the spiritual through the natural is like translating from a richer language into a poorer language. We have only the emotion of laughter to express the most foul obscenities and most Godly joy; we have only the emotion of tears to express the most selfish and worldly feelings and the most Godly sorrow. Therefore, we must not be unduly surprised that spiritual rejoicings are so similar in their outward manifestations as rejoicings of the more worldly kind.'[2]

For further study ▶

## FOR FURTHER STUDY

1. Read the high priestly prayer of Jesus in John 17, in which he asks that his followers 'may be one' (vv. 11, 21-23). How does this unity differ from the unity of the present-day ecumenical movement?

2. Under Zerubbabel and Jeshua, the Jews celebrated the Feast of Tabernacles. Read in Leviticus 23 about the different feasts; what do we learn about the meaning and purpose of them?

3. Read in Genesis 12-25 of six altars that are mentioned. What were the circumstances surrounding each one?

## TO THINK ABOUT AND DISCUSS

1. What are the things that promote unity in the local church? What practical steps do you think you and others could take to develop such unity?

2. Discuss the 'altar principle'; what can undermine it in our lives and homes?

3. What lessons can we learn from the history of the early church? Suggest both positive and negative ones.

4. What place should emotion have in worship?

# 4 Opposition to the work

(4:1-24)

Chapter three ended on a note of joy and celebration with the laying of the foundation of the temple. But this feeling of euphoria was short-lived...

With the opening of our present chapter we find God's people coming up against some stiff opposition to their building work. Not that it appeared as opposition at first, but more as a very friendly approach with an offer of help

## No compromise

Now when the adversaries of Judah and Benjamin heard that the descendants of the captivity were building the temple of the LORD God of Israel, they came to Zerubbabel and the heads of the fathers' houses, and said to them, "Let us build with you, for we seek your God as you do; and we have sacrificed to him since the days of Esarhaddon king of Assyria, who brought us here." But Zerubbabel and Jeshua and the rest of the heads of the fathers' houses of Israel said to them, "You may do nothing with us to build a house for our God; but we alone will build to the LORD God of Israel, as King Cyrus the king of Persia has commanded us" (4:1-3).

At a first reading it is difficult to understand why Zerubbabel, Jeshua and the other leaders were so adamant in their refusal to accept the offer of help by these people described as 'adversaries'. Why are they called this when they appear to be so kind and co-operative in spirit in wanting to join in this great work of building God's house? After all, they were not pagans but deeply religious people who worshipped the true God of Israel. They said, 'Let us build with you, for we seek your God as you do; and we have sacrificed to him...'.

Were the Jews being intolerant and ungracious in adopting this uncompromising attitude? Well, we must first ask who these people were. The answer is to be found in 2 Kings 17. When the ten northern tribes of Israel went into exile to Assyria in 721 B.C., Esarhaddon, the king of Assyria, sent some of his own people to colonize the depopulated areas. These Assyrians intermarried with the Jews who were left in Israel, creating a mixed population. And because Samaria was the administrative capital of the new colony, they became known as Samaritans. The result was that this mixture of Jews with Assyrians led to a mixture of true and false religion. 'They feared the LORD, yet served their own gods' (2 Kings 17:33).

We can now see why the Jews in Jerusalem refused to co-operate with the Samaritans. To allow them to share in the building of God's house would have jeopardized God's blessing upon the work.

That is the situation that still arises today when evangelical Christians are faced with approaches from the ecumenical movement to join in with the work of building the church in the world, but at the expense of compromising biblical truth and doctrine. Evangelicals can never go along with that, since for them reliance upon the truth and power of God's word alone is absolute if we are to halt the advance of the moral and spiritual decay in the life of our nations. Those of a liberal and ecumenical persuasion would consider that it was terribly sad and highly intolerant of Zerubbabel and the other leaders to reject the offer of help from the Samaritans, since they were not worldly godless people, but worshipped the true God of Israel, practised the same system of sacrifices, were gracious in their manner, and genuinely wanted to share in the building of God's house.

Surely that was enough to make them acceptable as fellow-believers, it might be thought? But that is to overlook the fact that they also worshipped other gods, thus making their religion a mixture of the true and the false. And God had made it perfectly clear in his law: 'You shall have no other gods before me' (Exod. 20:3). It was for this reason that the prophets of the Old Testament thundered against the 'false prophets', who outwardly appeared genuine enough since they spoke the prophetic language, worshipped God and wore the prophet's dress. But in reality they were doing the devil's work, and leading the people astray. Later, when speaking of the gospel, the Lord Jesus said that false prophets 'who come to you in sheep's clothing ... inwardly ... are ravenous wolves' (Matt. 7:15).

How are we to interpret that today unless as a direct warning against uniting with those who outwardly appear to be Christians; who worship God, are friendly and courteous, and genuinely want to share in the work of building God's kingdom in the world? For like the Samaritans, there are other ingredients in their faith that we must also take into account, and which betray the falseness of their position. They deny the total sufficiency of Scripture for life and doctrine, they dislike any talk of God's wrath and judgement, hell and destruction, the substitutionary death of Christ, man's total inability to do anything about his own salvation, and the physical resurrection of Christ. Instead, their 'gospel' is meant to be consumer-friendly and to make people feel good on the inside by saying little, if anything, about the exceeding sinfulness of the human heart. Spurgeon once described this kind of liberal preaching as using bits of the Bible as coat hangers on which to hang a few moral platitudes. God forbid that evangelicals should ever want to unite with that!

> Spurgeon once described ...liberal preaching as using bits of the Bible as coat hangers on which to hang a few moral platitudes. God forbid that evangelicals should ever want to unite with that!

In his useful little booklet *The Unresolved Controversy: unity with non-evangelicals*, Iain H. Murray quotes the following: 'William Warburton, Bishop of Gloucester, demanded of John Wesley, "Why do you talk of the success of the gospel in England, which was a Christian country before you were born?" to which Wesley replied, "Was it indeed? Is it so at this day? If men are not Christians till they are renewed after the image of Christ, and if the people of England, in general, are not so renewed, why do we term them so? The god of this world hath 'long blinded their hearts'. Let us do nothing to increase their blindness; but rather recover them from that strong delusion, that they may no longer believe a lie." '3

That still remains the evangelical position: to refuse any union that will blind people to God's truth and lead them into believing a lie.

## Opposition in the open

The moment Zerubbabel and his fellow-leaders made their position clear, the attitude of the Samaritans quickly changed from friendliness into open hostility. 'Then the people of the land tried to discourage the people of Judah. They troubled them in building, and hired counselors against them to frustrate their purpose all the days of Cyrus king of Persia, even until the reign of Darius king of Persia' (4:4-5).

Before dealing with this question of the opposition of the Samaritans to the building of the temple, we must clear up something that could cause confusion in people's minds. In verses 6-23 we have an account of the correspondence that passed between the surrounding people who opposed the rebuilding of Jerusalem and two later kings, Ahasuerus (Xerxes) and Artaxerxes. We may wonder why Ezra brings in this material at this juncture, since it breaks the continuity of the story of the building of the temple. The answer is that he is concerned to show the inveterate hatred of those who oppose God's work, whether in the building of the temple, or the later building of the city of Jerusalem. It is one and the same adversary, Satan, who is behind all opposition to God's work in every age and situation. He manipulates people to do his will.

As we read through the Bible it will quickly be seen that everyone who is engaged in God's work, and lives the Christian life sincerely, will sooner or later be confronted by opposition. Jesus warned us of that in the Beatitudes: 'Blessed are those who are persecuted for righteousness' sake, for theirs is the kingdom of heaven. Blessed are you when they revile and persecute you, and say all kinds of evil against you falsely for my sake' (Matt. 5:10-11). And Paul reminds us: 'All who desire to live godly in Christ Jesus will suffer persecution' (2 Tim. 3:12).

We can see from our present passage that when God's people are active in his work, in this instance building the temple, then Satan will be equally active in seeking to suppress it. And he will use every means at his disposal. Sometimes he will use subtlety, coming as 'an angel of light' (2 Cor. 11:14), as in the friendly approach of the Samaritans. At other times, his strategy is to prowl about 'like a roaring lion, seeking whom he may devour' (1 Peter 5:8). He will use friends and family, times of sadness and joy, times when things are going well with us, and times when circumstances are against us. But always his aim is the same: to undermine God's work in the world and to crush God's people. Make no mistake; Christians get the special attention of Satan. He studies us very closely, watching every move we make so as to bring us crashing down morally and spiritually.

## The character of opposition

We have already seen that Satan's opposition can take many forms. It is not for nothing that among the descriptions given of him in the Scriptures we read that he is 'a liar and the father of lies' (John 8:44, NIV), and 'the accuser of our brethren' (Rev. 12:10). The opposition to the rebuilding of the city of Jerusalem at a future stage took the form of slander and lying against both the workers and the work, In their letter to king Artaxerxes, the enemies of the Jews made the most vicious and false accusations. They attacked on three fronts.

FIRST, they impressed upon the king that to allow the city to be rebuilt would invite rebellion. 'Let it be known to the king that the Jews who came up from you have come to us at Jerusalem, and are building the rebellious and evil city, and are finishing its walls and repairing the foundations' (4:12). This was a vicious lie, since it was clearly obvious that the Jews were far too weak to entertain any idea of rebellion or seeking independence from the Persian king.

SECOND, they warned that if the city was rebuilt and fortified the king would lose revenue and taxes. 'Let it now be known to the king that, if this city is built and the walls completed, they will not pay tax, tribute, or custom, and the king's treasury will be diminished' (4:13). This too was a false accusation, since not only did the Jews continue to pay taxes and tribute, but later king Artaxerxes himself gave orders to Ezra that no taxes or tribute were to be imposed on the priests and Levites and the servants of the house of God (7:24).

**THIRD,** they warned that if Jerusalem was rebuilt the king would lose part of his kingdom beyond the river Euphrates. 'We inform the king that if this city is rebuilt and its walls are completed, the result will be that you will have no dominion beyond the River' (4:16). This was both a false and ridiculous accusation since, as we said earlier, the Jews were far too weak to think of expanding their borders, and in any case only once in history, during the reign of Solomon, did Israel's borders extend to the Euphrates (1 Kings 4:21).

> Satanic opposition to the work of God's kingdom is characterized by deceit, misrepresentation, lying and false accusation. We must expect that from the world.

The point we are making in all this is to show that satanic opposition to the work of God's kingdom is characterized by deceit, misrepresentation, lying and false accusation. We must expect that from the world. Satan accused Job of serving God out of self-interest. 'But now, stretch out your hand and touch all that he has, and he will surely curse you to your face!' (Job 1:11). But he was wrong. Job did not curse God. Satan falsely accused Stephen of blasphemy. 'They also set up false witnesses who said, "This man does not cease to speak blasphemous words against this holy place and the law" ' (Acts 6:13). And Satan attempted the same false accusation of Jesus at his trial. 'For many bore false witness against him, but their testimonies did not agree' (Mark 14:56).

So let us be on our guard, for, in this warfare of the Spirit, if Satan cannot gain advantage by accusing us outwardly, he will accuse us through our conscience. He will attack our motives; remind us of inner weaknesses; whisper that we are hypocrites not worthy to be God's children, and that God's grace in our lives is all an illusion. So the accusations will go on and on, for Satan never gives up. But we know that such accusations are false, for we have the witness of the Spirit within. 'The Spirit himself bears witness with our spirit that we are children of God' (Rom. 8:16).

## Short-term victory

When we come to the last verse in this chapter (v.24), we are back with Zerubbabel and Jeshua, and the opposition of the Samaritans to the building of the temple. Their continued harassment and correspondence with the Persian king had the desired effect. 'Thus the work of the house of God which is at Jerusalem ceased, and it was discontinued until the second year of the reign of Darius king of Persia.'

This cessation of the work, which lasted about sixteen years, would have been a great blow to the Jews, and they must have wondered in themselves if God's purpose had been defeated. Had all their work and sacrifice been in vain? Had Satan and the enemies of truth and righteousness won after all? Well, not quite. But we must look at this disturbing situation a little more closely.

To begin with, we have to accept the unpleasant fact that, in the warfare of the Spirit, Satan, working through the malignancy and sinfulness of fallen humanity—such as the Samaritans—does have his victories, and is able to frustrate the purposes of God. That is the negative aspect of the Christian warfare with the forces of darkness in the world. But on the positive side, we can take great comfort from the fact that Satan and the powers of evil can only frustrate the purposes of God in the *short term*. That is to say he can, and does, win a battle here and there, but he can never win the war itself. God is always in ultimate control. That is brought out very clearly in the book of Job. Satan could only do to Job what God's permissive will allowed him to do. 'And the LORD said to Satan, "Behold, all that he has is in your power; only do not lay a hand on his person." So Satan went out from the presence of the Lord' (Job 1:12).

This tells us that all the devil's stratagems to put a stop to God's work in the world always fail in the long run. Through his servant Isaiah God says, 'My counsel shall stand, and I will do all my pleasure' (Isa. 46:10). In the matter of building the temple, therefore, the opposition of the Samaritans, or the command of the Persian king to halt the work, or the sixteen years when nothing was done, would not determine the final outcome; only God himself would.

This will come out very clearly in our next chapter when, at the end of the sixteen years, when Darius I came to the Persian throne, he commanded that the work on God's house should be resumed and it was finally brought to completion. Unlike us, what God begins he always finishes. That surely is the central truth underlying Christ's death on the cross. To all outward appearances it seemed as if God's purpose in his Son was defeated, and the agents of evil had won the day. Even Christ's own followers on the Emmaus road thought it was the end of all their hopes: 'But we were hoping that it was he who was going to redeem Israel' (Luke 24:21). And then came Easter day and the resurrection and, far from being the end of God's purpose, it was the beginning of the new dispensation and the birth of God's church in the world. The last word is never with men but with God.

The important thing is that we should neither overestimate Satan's power, as if he were equal with God, nor underestimate his power and ability to manipulate people like the Samaritans to hinder God's work in the world. We said earlier that, as those who belong to the Lord Jesus Christ, we get the special attention of Satan. He watches us closely, assessing our strengths and weaknesses as he weighs up the best form of attack.

But for all his sinister power and cunning, he is a created being and therefore no match for the sovereign God who created him. Unlike us, God does not work in fits and starts, beginning a project, like building the temple, only to change his purpose and abandon his project further along the line. His purpose stands, and nothing that Satan and the demonic powers of this world can do can ever prevent it from coming to completion.

For further study ▶

## FOR FURTHER STUDY

1. Read 2 Kings 17:24-41. What light does this passage shed on the enmity between Jews and Samaritans?

2. Satan was behind the opposition to the building of the temple. Read Job 1:1 - 2:10 to see how powerful Satan is. Why does God allow Satan to afflict his people?

## TO THINK ABOUT AND DISCUSS

1. Does opposition to the gospel, in whatever form, hinder or help the cause of Christ in the world, or does it do both? Can you think of cases in Scripture to substantiate your response to this question?

2. When should Christians be prepared to compromise? When should they refuse?

3. What reasons do we have for believing that God's purpose always prevails in the long term?

4. Do you agree that we can both overestimate and underestimate Satan's power? What are the dangers in each case?

# 5 Two powerful preachers

(5:1 - 6:22)

Chapters 5 and 6 have to be taken together as they cover the same subject matter: the recommencement of the building of the temple during the reign of Darius king of Persia. When reading the Bible, we sometimes need to use a bit of sanctified imagination in order to visualize the situation we are reading about.

Imagine, then, the scene at the building site in Jerusalem after sixteen years had passed since any work had been done. The weeds and nettles had grown up over the foundation of the temple, which had been laid earlier, and the general impression was one of desolation and neglect.

In the meantime, the people returned to their own towns and villages, to care for their fields and complete the work of building their own houses. As the years passed, any thought of building God's house began to recede, and eventually the desire to do so died altogether. But then Darius I ascended the

Persian throne and suddenly, with the opening of chapter 5, the scene changed dramatically with the emergence of two very powerful preachers.

## Haggai and Zechariah

> Then the prophet Haggai and Zechariah the son of Iddo, prophets, prophesied to the Jews who were in Judah and Jerusalem, in the name of the God of Israel, who was over them. So Zerubbabel the son of Shealtiel and Jeshua the son of Jozadak rose up and began to build the house of God which is in Jerusalem; and the prophets of God were with them, helping them
> (5:1-2).

Who were these two prophets who preached to the people of Jerusalem and changed the situation so radically? We know quite a lot about them since each has a book named after him in the Bible. Haggai's book begins with the words: 'In the second year of King Darius, in the sixth month, on the first day of the month, the word of the LORD came by Haggai the prophet to Zerubbabel the son of Shealtiel, governor of Judah, and to Joshua the son of Jehozadak, the high priest' (Hag. 1:1). The book of Zechariah begins with the words: 'In the eighth month of the second year of Darius, the word of the LORD came to Zechariah the son of Berechiah, the son of Iddo the prophet' (Zech. 1:1).

So here were two men with a definite message from God concerning the rebuilding of the temple. Haggai's book contains the substance of that message, and we shall need to look at it more closely. Zechariah's book is more difficult to understand, and consists of a series of visions; but they, too, are directed to encouraging the people to complete the building of God's house.

## Prophetic preaching

If we stay with Haggai we can see that his message has a threefold emphasis.

First, he wants to rouse the people from the dreadful lethargy that seemed to have gripped them with the passing years. 'Thus speaks the LORD of hosts, saying: "This people says, 'The time has not come, the time that the LORD's house should be built' " ' (Hag. 1:2). If anyone during those sixteen years had raised the question: 'Do you not think we ought to do something about starting work on God's house again?', the people would have said, 'Oh the time is not right yet,' and then they would have come up with all sorts of excuses as to why that time was not right. In other words, a spirit of apathy and indolence had crept over them from which they could not seem to rouse themselves, and so the work of God remained at a standstill.

This was not something unique to the Jews of that time. We see a good deal of it in various walks of life today, especially in the political sphere. It fills politicians with despair that so many people cannot be bothered to vote at local and national elections. But it becomes especially serious on the spiritual front when this apathetic attitude creeps into the life of the church. Like some insidious disease it can permeate our spirit, and—unless there is a real effort of the will to shake it off—it can easily cause us to sink into an awful state of inertia where nothing gets done and God's work suffers.

For example, this feeling of lethargy can creep over us when we no longer attend God's house as regularly as we once did; or we are not seen as often at the prayer and Bible study meeting; or we are no longer consistent in our personal prayer-time and the reading of God's Word. And then someone or something may rouse our conscience and we tell ourselves we really must be more faithful at the worship services. But somehow—like the people of Haggai's day—the time to get active again never seems right, and we sink deeper into a state of indolence and indifference, and all the time God's work and God's house remain neglected.

What is needed is a determined effort of the will to exert more discipline on ourselves, and to start getting our spiritual life together again before it collapses altogether. The will plays an important part in Christian experience. To quote Frances Ridley Havergal's consecration hymn:

Take my will, and make it Thine;

It shall be no longer mine…4

Second, Haggai calls the people back to a right sense of priorities. 'Then the word of the LORD came by Haggai the prophet, saying, "Is it time for you yourselves to dwell in your panelled houses, and this temple to lie in ruins?" ' (Hag. 1:3-4).

That was a biting criticism of the people's priorities. It was as if God was saying to them: 'You say the time is not right to build my house. But I notice you give plenty of time to building and refurbishing your own houses with decorative panelling and other extras.' Not that it was wrong in any sense for the people to furnish their homes tastefully, and to provide themselves with certain comforts. The point Haggai was making was that these things had taken over their lives, and had become more important to them than the service of God. Their sense of priorities had become distorted.

And that can easily happen with us. Our homes and families, our jobs and careers, our interests and pleasures, can all displace and jeopardize the work of God in our lives to the extent that even God himself becomes marginalized. It is both sad and serious when that happens, because it means we are then living at a shallow spiritual level with little hope of growing in our faith. Our Lord warns us about this in his Parable of the Sower: 'Now these are the ones sown among thorns; they are the ones who hear the word, and the cares of this world, the deceitfulness of riches, and the desires for other things entering in choke the word, and it becomes unfruitful' (Mark 4:18-19).

What happens is that our life can get so crowded with other things, so cluttered up with other concerns, that there is no time or room for reflection upon the things of the soul, and the Holy Spirit has to compete with all these other things to get a foothold in our lives. The gospel is not the all-embracing experience it should be for the Christian. And that has serious consequences, as Haggai goes on to explain.

Third, he warns the people that they are losing out as long as God's house and God's work remain neglected:

Now therefore, thus says the LORD of hosts: "Consider your ways!

You have sown much, and bring in little;

You eat, but do not have enough;

You drink, but you are not filled with drink;

You clothe yourselves, but no one is warm;

And he who earns wages,

Earns wages to put into a bag with holes."

Thus says the LORD of hosts: "Consider your ways! Go up to the mountains and bring wood and build the temple, that I may take pleasure in it and be glorified," says the LORD (Hag. 1:5-8).

It is as if God is saying to the people: 'Where has all this concentration and effort upon your own concerns got you in the end? Are you any happier, or more contented, or more at peace in your hearts? No, because I have withheld my blessing from you because you have neglected me and the work of my house. I have withheld the harvests, and what little money you have is eaten up with inflation, like putting it into a bag with holes.'

The lesson is clear. When we marginalize God and neglect his work, he removes his blessing, and our lives become spiritually impoverished. In short, we lose out. I believe that is largely the explanation for the poor quality of spiritual life in the UK today. For many years now, the church has not truly honoured God in the faithful preaching of his Word. Worldliness has seeped into church life to such an extent that we are now partly under the judgement of God by the removal of his blessing. Even in those churches where pastors are working hard and are faithfully preaching the gospel, we are not seeing conversions. There are exceptions, of course, but generally speaking the overall picture is not an inspiring one.

What the answer is to this state of affairs I am not sure. But in the light of this passage I feel that God may be saying to us, as he said to the Jews of Jerusalem, 'Consider your ways!' They did exactly that, and considered Haggai's warning seriously. 'Then Zerubbabel the son of Shealtiel, and Joshua the son of Jehozadak, the high priest, with all the remnant of the people, obeyed the voice of the Lord their God, and the words of Haggai the prophet, as the Lord their God had sent him … and they came and worked on the house of the Lord of hosts, their God' (Hag. 1:12, 14).

## Satan never gives up

We are now back in Ezra. The work recommenced with great energy and purposefulness, but it was not to last. Within a couple of months, the opposition from the surrounding peoples was active once more. This time it was led by Tattenai, a high official of the Persian king. 'At the same time Tattenai the governor of the region beyond the River and Shethar-Boznai and their companions came to them and spoke thus to them: "Who has commanded you to build this temple and finish this wall?" ' (5:3).

Although Zerubbabel and the other leaders assured them that such authorization had been granted sixteen years before by King Cyrus (5:13-14), they were not satisfied and wrote a letter of complaint to king Darius. The remainder of chapter 5 from verse 6 is taken up with the contents of this letter, but we need only point out that it ends with a request that a search be made in the royal archives to see if Cyrus had in fact given such authorization. 'Now therefore, if it seems good to the king, let a search be made in the king's treasure house, which is there in Babylon, whether it is so that a decree was issued by King Cyrus to build this house of God at Jerusalem, and let the king send us his pleasure concerning this matter' (5:17).

There now followed an anxious time for the Jews. We can imagine how all the old fears and frustrations must have gripped their hearts as they waited for the king's reply. Would the work of God be brought to a standstill yet again?

Clearly what we learn from this is that Satan never gives up in his efforts to frustrate the ongoing work of God in the world. We learned earlier that in the Christian life we are to expect opposition from the enemy of our souls. But when it confronts us, and we are enabled with God's help to resist it successfully, we must never think that is the end of the matter. We must never fall into the trap of thinking that we are finished with the devil's opposition because we gained a victory over him at some point. He will always come back to the attack, and if we are not ready for him he will take us by surprise and undermine our defences.

Ours is a constant battle with the forces of evil at work in the world. It goes on from one circumstance to another, from age to age and from generation to generation. And it will never cease until the final battle, when the Lord Jesus returns to this earth and finally destroys the devil and all his works. So let us be on our guard. Peter urges us: 'Be sober, be vigilant; because your adversary the devil walks about like a roaring lion, seeking whom he may devour. Resist him, steadfast in the faith' (1 Peter 5:8-9).

## The wonderful ways of God

As we move into chapter 6 the situation changes yet again, but this time for the better. In verses 1-5 we learn that a search was made in the archives in Babylon and a scroll was discovered containing the original decree of Cyrus for the building of the temple. Then, from verse 6 onwards, we have the reply of King Darius to Tattenai. This is an amazing document from a pagan king, for he comes down solidly on the side of God and his people: 'Now therefore, Tattenai, governor of the region beyond the River, and Shethar-Boznai, and your companions the Persians who are beyond the River, keep yourselves far from there. Let the work of this house of God alone; let the governor of the Jews and the elders of the Jews build this house of God on its site' (6:6-7).

This in itself was marvellous news for God's people. But Darius goes a lot further:

> Moreover I issue a decree as to what you shall do for the elders of these Jews, for the building of this house of God: Let the cost be paid at the king's expense from taxes on the region beyond the River; this is to be given immediately to these men, so that they are not hindered. And whatever they need—young bulls, rams, and lambs for the burnt offerings of the God of heaven, wheat, salt, wine, and oil, according to the request of the priests who are in Jerusalem—let it be given them day by day without fail
>
> (6:8-9).

And then comes the most amazing statement of all: 'That they may offer sacrifices of sweet aroma to the God of heaven, and pray for the life of the king and his sons' (6:10).

God's people must have been 'over the moon' when they heard all this! How wonderful are God's ways! The apostle Paul is so right when he says: 'Oh, the depth of the riches both of the wisdom and knowledge of God! How unsearchable are his judgements and his ways past finding out!' (Rom. 11:33). Who would have thought that such a desperate situation facing God's people could change so radically? It was all God's doing. We cannot always explain the ways of God with his people, but the comforting truth is that we do not need to *explain* God, but only *trust* him; believe that when the situation demands he can move a pagan king like Cyrus to *begin* his work, and another pagan king like Darius to *finish* that work. 'Now the temple was finished on the third day of the month of Adar [March], which was in the sixth year of the reign of King Darius. Then the children of Israel, the priests and the Levites and the rest of the descendants of the captivity, celebrated the dedication of this house of God with joy' (6:15-16).

> If we believe that God answers prayer, we must show that, to us, it is a meaningful reality. It is not talking to the air, but holding communion with a personal, loving, heavenly father.

## The reality of prayer

What I find of deep significance in the decree of Darius is his request that God's people should pray for him and his family. 'That they may offer sacrifices of sweet aroma to the God of heaven, and pray for the life of the king and his sons' (6:10). After all, he was a pagan king, with little, if any, understanding and knowledge of the true and living God. But this should not surprise us, since man is a spiritual being, created in the image of God, and every once in a while—especially in a time of crisis—that spiritual dimension will cause a person to reach out beyond the material world to the spiritual.

During the Second World War there was a common saying among the Allied armed forces: 'there are no atheists in foxholes'. This meant that when a man in combat is hiding in a hole in the ground with shells bursting all around him, he would suddenly find himself praying even though he had never prayed in his life before. And, like any other pastor, I have been visiting in a hospital when someone has reached out a hand and said, 'Please say a prayer for me.' Why do people do that, when normally it would never enter their minds to pray? Is it a belief in a form of magic, or a psychological release, or do they do it because everything else has failed? I do not know, but since as Christians we believe in the reality of prayer, we ought not to treat any such request lightly but use it as a form of witness.

When Hudson Taylor was a young man sailing from Liverpool to China as a missionary on the ship 'Dumfries' in 1835, he had a similar experience. After some weeks, the ship was becalmed off the coast of New Guinea and in danger of being dragged by a powerful undercurrent towards a hidden reef. The longboat was launched and attached to the ship by ropes in an attempt to change direction, but this failed. Then the captain, a non-Christian, said to Hudson Taylor, a mere boy of twenty-two, 'you believe in a God who answers prayer; pray that he will save us'. Hudson Taylor went below and prayed, and after a while the wind came up, filling the sails and driving the ship out of danger.

If we believe that God answers prayer, we must show that, to us, it is a meaningful reality. It is not talking to the air, but holding communion with a personal, loving, heavenly father.

### An even greater work

During the years God's people were working on building the temple, beneath the surface an even greater work was going on in the hearts of the surrounding peoples—the work of salvation. When the worship of the temple was established, the Jews celebrated by keeping the Passover. 'And the descendants of the captivity kept the Passover on the fourteenth day of the first month' (6:19).

But, more importantly, we read in verse 21: 'Then the children of Israel who had returned from the captivity ate together with all who had separated themselves from the filth of the nations of the land in order to seek the LORD God of Israel.' Those who 'separated themselves' were Gentiles converted from paganism to the worship of the true and living God.

What drew them from the worship of their false gods to the God of Israel? We are not told specifically, but the faithfulness of the Jews, and their obedience to the call of God to build his house, must have borne its own witness. After all, it is not only through preaching that men and women are brought to salvation. It is a work that is going on all the time in various ways. God uses our faithfulness and obedience, and our words and actions, as a witness to others. And even when we ourselves are not fully aware of it, the silent operations of the Holy Spirit are all the time opening the eyes of people's understanding to bring them to see the glory of God in the face of Jesus Christ.

## FOR FURTHER STUDY

1. Read Haggai and get a deeper insight into the building of God's house in Ezra.

2. In conjunction with the section 'Satan never gives up', read of the temptations of Jesus in Luke 4 to see the truth of that. Can you think of another time when Satan returned to tempt Jesus?

3. For an example of God's delay in answering prayer, read of John the Baptist's birth in Luke 1:5-13.

## TO THINK ABOUT AND DISCUSS

1. What do you consider to be powerful preaching? In what ways does it help and challenge people?

2. Discuss the question of 'priorities' in the life of the Christian. What do you think can be done to help people to set their priorities in a way that accords with the central emphases of Scripture?

3. Satan never gives up. What examples have you seen of this in your experience? How should we prepare for his attack?

4. Discuss, in the light of your own experience, the 'wonderful ways of God'.

5. Are there times when we feel constrained to pray with others when they ask us to do so? And are there times when we do not feel constrained to do so?

6. What are the different ways in which we can witness to others?

# 6 Ezra arrives on the scene

(7:1-28)

In our last chapter we learned that the temple in Jerusalem was completed in the sixth year of the reign of Darius the Persian king in about 516 B.C. The leading figures in that work of restoration—Zerubbabel the governor, Jeshua the high priest, and the prophets Haggai and Zechariah—are no longer around by the time we get to chapter 7.

Some sixty years have now passed, during which Xerxes, a new king (486-464), has come to the throne and has been succeeded by Artaxerxes (464-425); he is the king in this chapter, and it is during his reign that Ezra himself appears on the scene, leading another group of exiles back to Jerusalem. 'Now after these things, in the reign of Artaxerxes king of Persia, Ezra the son of Seraiah … came up from Babylon; and he was a skilled scribe in the Law of Moses, which the LORD God of Israel had given. The king granted him all his request, according to the hand of the LORD his God upon him' (7:1, 6).

## Ezra loved God's Word

Jewish tradition has a great deal to say about Ezra. It claims that he established the system of synagogue worship while in Babylon, that he played an important part in the formation of the Old Testament canon, and wrote the books of Chronicles, Nehemiah and Esther. The historicity of these claims is by no means established, but the very fact that they are attributed to Ezra shows us something of the greatness of the man, and why in Jewish tradition he is regarded as a second Moses.

But the one thing we can say with absolute certainty about Ezra is that he loved God's Word. We read in verse 10, 'For Ezra had prepared his heart to seek the Law of the LORD, and to do it, and to teach statutes and ordinances in Israel.'

Notice the three things we are told here about Ezra's attitude to God's Word. He was prepared to seek it, to study it; he did it, he put it into practice; and he was concerned to teach it to others. Let us look at each of these.

**FIRST**, the study of God's Word was no irksome task to Ezra; it was his joy and delight. He was devoted to it. We are told that he was a 'skilled scribe in the Law of Moses' (v. 6). The psalmist's description of the godly man fits Ezra perfectly. 'But his delight is in the law of the LORD, and in his law he meditates day and night' (Ps. 1:2). As he studied the word, Ezra was conscious that behind the sacred writings there was the authority of the living God, revealing his will and purpose for his people.

What does this say to us about the time we are prepared to give to the reading and study of God's Word? Is the Bible precious to us? Do we read it in such a way as to allow it to sift and search our hearts, and to illuminate our minds with its mighty truths? Far too many Christians are content simply to read a few verses of the Bible whenever the fancy takes them. But that is not good enough if we are to feed our souls and minds on God's Word. It is when we seriously search the Scriptures, with a desire to learn and understand, that the Holy Spirit comes to our aid. When the Lord Jesus spoke to the disciples in the upper room we are told: 'He opened their understanding, that they might comprehend the Scriptures' (Luke 24:45).

> Far too many Christians are content simply to read a few verses of the Bible whenever the fancy takes them. But that is not good enough if we are to feed our souls and minds on God's Word.

Pastors and preachers, too, should give time to reading the Bible devotionally for the good of their own souls, otherwise it becomes no more than a textbook which they study in a detached and professional way for the making of sermons. I say it sadly, but I have been in the Christian ministry long enough to detect, even among evangelical Christians, a considerable lessening in the understanding of the Bible as God's Word.

**SECOND,** we are told that, where God's Word was concerned, Ezra prepared his heart 'to do it'. In other words, he obeyed it, and applied its teaching and principles to daily life. The Bible is not meant to be read or studied for intellectual and spiritual enjoyment alone, but is meant to be lived out in all the circumstances of daily life. As the psalmist says, 'Your word is a lamp to my feet and a light to my path' (Ps. 119:105). Its teachings are meant to guide us along the perplexing paths of life, to lay down principles of conduct, to help us with our difficulties, and to impart comfort in times of distress.

There are Christians who like to spend all their time talking about the Bible, and discussing the finer points of doctrine, but who never actually begin to live it. And let us face it: in the end, living the life is what a large part of the gospel is all about. People must see that we live a different set of values and standards. So if the Word of God is to do its work in the hearts and minds of men and women, there must come a point where we stop verbalizing and pontificating about it, and start applying it. Others may then see that our Christian faith is not a lot of 'phoney chatter', but is relevant to life in the modern world.

THIRD, we are told that where God's Word was concerned, Ezra desired 'to teach [its] statutes and ordinances in Israel'. That is, he studied God's Word in order to become competent in teaching it to others. When we get to chapter 9 we shall see that Ezra brought about a reformation in Israel because the people had backslidden. He could never have done this without applying the Word of God and exercising its authority.

In the book of Nehemiah we have a wonderful picture of Ezra, standing on a high platform or pulpit, opening up the Scriptures and explaining their meaning to the people: 'So Ezra the scribe stood on a platform of wood which they had made for the purpose... And Ezra opened the book in the sight of all the people, for he was standing above all the people; and when he opened it, all the people stood up. And Ezra blessed the LORD, the great God. Then all the people answered, "Amen, Amen!" while lifting up their hands. And they bowed their heads and worshiped the LORD with their faces to the ground' (Neh. 8:4-6). This was Ezra preaching.

### The privilege of preaching

It was Thomas Watson, the Puritan, who once said: 'God had only one son, and he made him a preacher.' And it was Samuel Chadwick who once declared, 'I would rather preach than do anything else in this world. I have never missed a chance to preach; I would rather preach than eat my dinner, or have a holiday or anything else the world can offer.' Those of us who are preachers should ask ourselves honestly, 'Do I love preaching God's Word?' and then follow it up with: 'Do I believe in the preaching of God's Word?'

> Unless it is evident to the members of the congregation that we believe in the message we preach, then it is not likely to do much for them.

For unless it is evident to the members of the congregation that we believe in the message we preach, then it is not likely to do much for them. There is nothing that will give a deeper sense of urgency and earnestness to a preacher, and put an edge on his preaching, than his own awareness that what he is doing originated with the Lord Jesus who called him to the work. Like the apostle Paul the preacher should 'magnify' his ministry, but never 'magnify' himself (Rom. 11:13). Three times in this chapter Ezra tells us that 'the hand of the LORD his God [was] upon him' (7:6,9,28). That is his way of saying that he knew he was God's man to teach his Word.

May we who are preachers have that same inward conviction and certainty that God's hand is upon us as we preach the way of salvation.

### The king's letter

In verse 6 we have this statement: 'The king granted him all his request, according to the hand of the LORD his God upon him.' That, of course, is a reference to the request Ezra made to king Artaxerxes to allow him to return to Jerusalem with a second group of exiles. The second half of this chapter is now taken up with the contents of the king's letter giving Ezra his authorization.

'This is a copy of the letter that King Artaxerxes gave Ezra the priest, the scribe, expert in the words of the commandments of the Lord, and of his statutes to Israel' (7:11). The letter extends from verse 12 to verse 26 and is a remarkable document. Its main points are as follows:

**VERSE 13**: Any of the king's subjects who were of Israelite descent were free to return to Jerusalem.

**VERSES 15-20**: Finances for the expedition and for the worship of God's house were to come from the royal treasury, and from the freewill offerings of those Jews remaining in Babylon.

**VERSE 19**: Ezra was to take with him the articles of gold and bronze donated by the king for use in the temple worship (see also 8:25).

**VERSE 24**: All God's servants consecrated to the work of

God's house were to be exempt from paying taxes.

**VERSES 25 AND 26**: Ezra was given authority to appoint magistrates and judges, and to enforce legal decisions with penalties of imprisonment, confiscation of goods, and even the death penalty.

As an expression of pagan piety, this letter, like the proclamations we saw earlier, is truly remarkable. Ezra himself acknowledged that, for the chapter ends with him giving thanks to God for the king's favour. 'Blessed be the LORD God of our fathers, who has put such a thing as this in the king's heart, to beautify the house of the LORD which is in Jerusalem, and has extended mercy to me before the king and his counsellors, and before all the king's mighty princes. So I was encouraged, as the hand of the LORD my God was upon me; and I gathered leading men of Israel to go up with me' (7:27-28).

## The Christian and public life

Ezra was in no doubt that it was God, in his overruling sovereignty, who had put it into the king's heart to be so favourably disposed towards him and the work to which God had called him. 'Blessed be the LORD God of our fathers, who has put such a thing as this in the king's heart' (7:27).

But we must not forget that, whereas God ordains the end of his providence, he also ordains the means by which that end may be accomplished. In this instance, the means used were the godly lives of many of the Jewish exiles, which must have had a powerful influence upon the Persian kings. Many of them held high office in the Persian court. Daniel was the second ruler in the kingdom under Cyrus and Darius;

Zerubbabel was appointed governor of Jerusalem by Cyrus; Nehemiah was cup-bearer to King Artaxerxes and later governor of Jerusalem. And Ezra himself, apart from being priest and scribe, must also have held an official position since Artaxerxes authorized him to appoint judges and magistrates, and even to carry out the death penalty.

It was the godliness and purity of the lives of these men, and the strength of their convictions in refusing to accommodate themselves to the pressures and standards of Babylonian culture, that made them instruments God could use to shape the thinking of these pagan kings, and to affect the course of Israel's history.

> It was the godliness and purity of the lives of these men, and the strength of their convictions in refusing to accommodate themselves to the pressures and standards of Babylonian culture, that made them instruments God could use...

That surely has something to say to us about the role Christians can play in public and political life. In his letter to the Romans, Paul clearly teaches that the civil authority is ordained by God, and everyone is subject to it. 'Let every soul be subject to the governing authorities. For there is no authority except from God, and the authorities that exist are appointed by God. Therefore whoever resists the authority resists the ordinance of God, and those who resist will bring judgement on themselves' (Rom. 13:1-2).

What Paul is saying corresponds with the words of Jesus himself when he said, 'Render to Caesar the things that are Caesar's and to God the things that are God's' (Mark 12:17). Caesar, or the state, *does* have its claims upon us, and it can make a tremendous difference when Christians respond positively to those claims. Indeed, the very fact that we hear so much today of bribery, corruption and immorality in public life shows just how far we have fallen from the scriptural teaching that government and its authority is derived from God. What is needed, therefore, is for more Christians to share in the exercise of that authority by playing an active part in public and political life.

And even when we are not ourselves actively involved in the political process, we are nevertheless urged in the Word of God to pray for those who are in authority over us (1 Tim. 2:1-2).

This is because Christians who are in positions of responsibility in public and political life can find themselves under acute pressure as they seek to apply the principles of the gospel. So often, in the rough and tumble of public life, conscience clashes with expediency, and conviction is challenged by compromise, and those caught up in it need the prayers of fellow-believers.

### The God of heaven

It is significant, I feel, that Artaxerxes in his letter uses the expression, 'the God of heaven' four times (7:12, 21 and 23). Remember this is a pagan king! We might have expected him to use an expression like 'the God of the Jews'. But to speak of the God of heaven suggests that the king had some notion, however vague, of a divine being and power who ruled over the destinies of men and nations, and who was infinitely greater than any of his own Babylonian deities.

And today, likewise, modern man is a creature of destiny. God created him with a spiritual dimension to his being, so that he is never fully satisfied with the things of this world, and there will always be times when he reaches out beyond himself for an explanation of his own existence. Like Artaxerxes, he feels instinctively that there are powers and forces at work in the universe which rule and govern the destinies of people and nations. It is true that his notions of this power in the heavens are crude and vague, as may be seen in the thousands, perhaps millions, who study their horoscopes, consult astrologers, and visit mediums and fortune-tellers. But why do they do it? It is because they are looking for some kind of assurance concerning their destiny.

Speaking of our search for meaning in life, the author of Ecclesiastes says that God 'has put eternity in their hearts, except that no one can find out the work that God does from beginning to end' (Eccles. 3:11). But the Christian *does* know what God's work and purpose is from beginning to end, and he wants to make it known to others. Nor is this purpose a vague, undefined feeling that there is something 'up there', or 'out there', but it is positive, personal and knowable. It is the eternal, living God who has revealed his mercy and grace in the person of his own dear son, the Lord Jesus Christ, and has made known his unfathomable purpose in the written word of Holy Scripture.

For further study ▶

## FOR FURTHER STUDY

1. Read Nehemiah 8 to get a true flavour of how deeply Ezra loved God's Word and taught it to the people.

2. Both Ezra and Nehemiah held an important position in public life as governor of Judah. Read of Joseph's role in public life in Genesis 41:41-49; Daniel's role, in Daniel 2:46-49; and the conversion of a Roman statesman, Sergius Paulus, in Acts 13:4-12.

## TO THINK ABOUT AND DISCUSS

1. Discuss the importance of personal Bible study; from your own experience, when do you think is the best time for it? How long should we spend on it? What is the best method?

2. We need more Christian men and women in responsible positions in public and political life. Do you agree with this statement? How can we support and encourage those who are in these positions?

3. Many today get involved in aspects of the occult—Satanism, spiritism, astrology, etc. What does this tell us about man's nature? How can we capitalize on it for evangelistic purposes?

# 7 Preparation for the journey

(8:1-36)

The first part of this chapter (vv. 1-14) contains yet another catalogue of names—this time of those exiles who accompanied Ezra on the second journey back to Jerusalem: 'These are the heads of their father's houses, and this is the genealogy of those who went up with me from Babylon, in the reign of King Artaxerxes' (8:1).

## Redemptive history

We may again wonder to ourselves, when reading this passage, why writers like Ezra were concerned to give us these long genealogies containing the names of people we know nothing about. But that is to misunderstand their purpose, and the place they have in the unfolding history of God's people. We must never forget that the history of the Bible is redemptive history, and these family records are meant to show us that God has preserved the promised line of the Messiah from generation to generation.

For example, in the Gospels we have two genealogies of Jesus. Matthew, writing for Jewish readers, traces the history of Jesus back to King David, and ultimately to Abraham as the father of the Jewish people (Matt. 1:1-17). Luke, on the other hand, was writing for Gentiles, and was concerned to show Jesus as the Saviour of mankind. He therefore traces the history of Jesus from Joseph, through David and back to 'Adam, the son of God' (Luke 3:23-38).

Another purpose of the biblical genealogies, which we saw earlier, is to enable us to see, in their generation-to-generation linkage, the fulfilment of the many messianic prophecies relating to Jesus. For example, God said to Abraham: 'I will make you a great nation … And in you all the families of the earth shall be blessed' (Gen. 12:2-3). Matthew begins his genealogy of Jesus with the fulfilment of that prophecy: 'The book of the genealogy of Jesus Christ, the Son of David, the Son of Abraham' (Matt. 1:1).

## The fading vision

Ezra's list of the returning exiles makes interesting reading if only because the total number comes to fewer than 1,500. This raises the same question we asked when considering the first return in chapter 2. Why so few? Back then, the number was about 50,000, but even that was small in comparison with the large number of Jews living in Babylon. On this second occasion the number was considerably smaller. Why was that?

We suggested earlier that life in Babylon had become so

secure and comfortable that many of the Jews had no desire to undertake the long, difficult journey back to Jerusalem and to face all the problems associated with rebuilding their homes and continuing God's work. I believe the same was true on this occasion. But now there was another, deeper reason. Sixty years had passed and the vision they once had of themselves as God's chosen people called to do his work, and to be his witness to the surrounding Gentile nations, had now faded almost to nothingness. They had lost the glow, and the zeal they once had was spent as they became increasingly absorbed into the culture and lifestyle of Babylon.

> God's chosen people ... had lost the glow, and the zeal they once had was spent as they became increasingly absorbed into the culture and lifestyle of Babylon.

Could that happen to us in our Christian lives? It most certainly can if we are not sufficiently alert. It was the very rebuke the risen Lord gave to the church in Ephesus: 'I have this against you, that you have left your first love' (Rev. 2:4). And in our personal lives the passing years can be cruel, and rob us of our Christian joy and our first love for Christ. It was a cause of great sadness to the apostle Paul when he wrote to Timothy: 'Demas has forsaken me, having loved this present world' (2 Tim. 4:10). We are citizens of two worlds; this world with its joys and pleasures, and that other eternal world to which we are drawing closer in Christ with every passing day. And always this world is seeking to cloud our spiritual vision, and to seduce us from our love for Christ and our hope of heaven.

## Ezra gets organized

A few days out on the journey from Babylon, and Ezra calls a halt at the river Ahava. 'Now I gathered them by the river that flows to Ahava, and we camped there three days. And I looked among the people and the priests, and found none of the sons of Levi there' (8:15).

The Ahava was a tributary of the river Euphrates, and Ezra had a twofold purpose in mind when he decided to camp there for three days. First, he wanted to make a final assessment of the situation before setting out on a journey of 900 miles, along difficult terrain and with the possibility of encountering formidable dangers from bandits. He spells this out on his arrival at Jerusalem. 'And the hand of our God was upon us, and he delivered us from the hand of the enemy and from ambush along the road' (8:31).

It was a good thing Ezra did make a final assessment because, on checking the exiles, he discovered there was not a single Levite among them. 'And I looked among the people and the priests, and found none of the sons of Levi there.' Was this significant in any way? I believe it was, or else why would Ezra mention it? Moreover, he considered it important enough to send to a nearby settlement for some of the Levites to join them.

And I gave them a command for Iddo the chief man at the place Casiphia ... that they should bring us servants for the house of our God. Then, by the good hand of our God upon us, they brought us a man of understanding, of the sons of

Mahli the son of Levi, the son of Israel, namely Sherebiah, with his sons and brothers, eighteen men; and Hashabiah, and with him Jeshaiah of the sons of Merari, his brothers and their sons, twenty men; also of the Nethinim, whom David and the leaders had appointed for the service of the Levites, two hundred and twenty Nethinim. All of them were designated by name
(8:17-20).

## Failure in leadership

So Ezra got his Levites eventually, but the incident points very forcefully to a failure on the part of the people's leaders. According to Deuteronomy 10:8-9, and Numbers chapters 3 and 4, the Levites were set apart before the Lord to minister to him, to serve in the temple and to bless the people. They were spiritual leaders, and should have been the very ones in the forefront supporting Ezra in the movement back to Jerusalem.

This failure on the part of God's official representatives was not something peculiar to Ezra's day. In the Bible we find that God sometimes bypassed the official leaders because of their failure, and raised up others to do his work. Eli and his sons Hophni and Phinehas were official priests, but, because of their failure to lead the people aright, God passed them by in favour of the boy Samuel (1 Sam. 2 and 3). Amos was a sheep farmer, but God raised him up as his spokesman because Amaziah the official priest was a spiritual disaster (Amos 7:10-17). In the New Testament it was not the Scribes, Pharisees and Sadducees—the religious leaders—whom God chose to be the foundation of his church, but a group of ordinary fishermen.

And in the history of the church we see the same thing. When the church needed reforming in the sixteenth century because of the abuses in the institutional leadership, God raised up an obscure monk in Martin Luther. Before the evangelical awakening of the eighteenth century, the worldliness of the bishops and clergy was destroying the spiritual life of the church, but God had his men in John and Charles Wesley, George Whitefield, Daniel Rowland, Howel Harris and others.

Today, we are again seeing this failure in the church's established leaders. But God has no vested interest in the establishment. If it fails in its calling, God will pass it by and raise up others. And that in fact is what is happening. Liberalism and political correctness have so infected the church's leadership that the hungry sheep look up and are not fed. When Jesus spoke about the Good Shepherd (John 10), he described the false shepherd as a thief and a robber. In the church today, false shepherds are robbing members of the congregation of the truth of God by substituting their own ideas and opinions for the Bible's teaching. But God's work will not fail. The Lord Jesus said, 'I will build my church, and the gates of Hades shall not prevail against it' (Matt. 16:18). If the Levites are not leading, God will raise up others to carry on the work.

## Waiting upon God

The other reason Ezra called a three-day halt at the Ahava River was to provide an opportunity for fasting, prayer and waiting upon God in preparation for the journey. 'Then I proclaimed a fast there at the river of Ahava, that we might humble ourselves before our God, to seek from him the right way for us and our little ones and all our possessions' (8:21).

James Philip, in his booklet *A time to build*,[5] says that 'Waiting time is never wasted time'. How right he is. Sometimes, in the Christian life, waiting is more important than running, or doing, or serving, or working, or anything else we might do. Ours is a frenetic age, and the pace of life is such that many of us, even in evangelical circles, no longer know how to 'wait' or 'be still' or 'meditate' in God's presence. Instead, we are overactive and would rather be running around, busy with a thousand and one other things in our Christian lives, than simply waiting in quietness upon God for help, illumination and strengthening.

As to fasting, it is not generally practised these days among Christians. But it is not actually commanded anywhere in the Bible except on the Day of Atonement, when the whole nation repented of its sins (see Lev. 16:29). Indeed, one of the criticisms made of Jesus was that he and his disciples did not fast like John the Baptist and his followers (Mark 2:18). But the principle underlying fasting is perfectly valid. It is to get away from all other distractions, including the preparation of food, in order to wait upon God.

## Jealous for God's honour

One other important reason for the time of prayer and fasting at the Ahava river was in order that Ezra could plead with God for special protection on the journey to Jerusalem—'to seek from him the right way for us and our little ones and all our possessions' (8:21). It seems he had debated within himself whether to ask King Artaxerxes for a military escort, but then decided against it. And he is humble and honest enough to tell us why. 'For I was ashamed to request of the king an escort of soldiers and horsemen to help us against the enemy on the road, because we had spoken to the king saying, "The hand of our God is upon all those for good who seek him, but his power and his wrath are against all those who forsake him". So we fasted and entreated our God for this, and he answered our prayer' (8:22-23).

We get the impression that, at the Ahava, Ezra was having second thoughts about the wisdom of not requesting a military escort in view of what lay ahead. Travel in those ancient times was extremely dangerous, and in addition to 1,500 men he had the women and children to think of, and the immense amount of treasure for God's house in the gifts from the king and his counsellors and the Jews remaining in Babylon (8:25). But he had already told the king that he had absolute confidence that 'the hand of our God is upon all those for good who seek him'. He felt he could not go back on that now by requesting a military escort. He was jealous for God's honour. That was real courage and daring, and great faith, to my mind. And God honoured it by bringing the whole company safely to Jerusalem: 'Then we departed from the river of Ahava on the twelfth day of the first month, to go to Jerusalem. And the hand of our God was upon us, and he delivered us from the hand of the enemy and from ambush along the road. So we came to Jerusalem, and stayed there three days' (8:31-32).

## Doing the daring thing

What do we learn from this? Well, it shows us that

sometimes, just sometimes, it might rejoice God's heart if we were to do something really daring for him; to throw all caution and prudence to the wind and launch out with nothing to go on but naked faith in his power to watch over us. I am not advocating recklessness, but simply willingness, when the occasion demands, to show some Holy Spirit boldness. Think of Daniel praying with his window wide open for everyone to see, when he knew the king had signed the decree against it (Dan. 6:10). Was that a cautious and prudent thing to do? Or take Paul, going back into the city when the mob there had already stoned him and left him for dead (Acts 14:19-20). Was that sensible?

The truth is that if the principle of caution and prudence must always, in all circumstances, guide our Christian lives, then we would never have had a single missionary in times past to plant the gospel in a foreign country, or thousands to live out their faith today in countries where they face continual persecution. We need to pray in the words of the hymn:

Lo! the hosts of evil round us

Scorn Thy Christ, assail His ways!

Fears and doubts too long have bound us;

Free our hearts to work and praise.

Grant us wisdom,

Grant us courage,

For the living of these days.[6]

For further study ▶

## FOR FURTHER STUDY

1. In Babylon, many of the Jews had lost the vision of their calling as God's people. Read the life of Lot in Genesis 13:1-13 and chapter 19 for another sad example of this. Also, read Revelation 2:1-5, and 2 Timothy 4:10.

2. What makes a good leader in God's work? Read 1 Timothy 3:1-13; Titus 1:5-9; 1 Peter 5:1-4.

## TO THINK ABOUT AND DISCUSS

1. In what ways do you think we can benefit from reading the genealogies in the Bible? Is there anything we can do to help ourselves gain even more benefit from them?

2. Not every Christian can be a good speaker, or a dynamic leader, etc. But no Christian can be excused a lack of zeal or lack of enthusiasm for Christ. Why is this?

3. Is there a failure of leadership in the church today? If so, how does it manifest itself? What is the cause, and what do you think can be done to remedy the situation?

4. In what ways can we be too timid in our Christian lives? Remember Paul's word to Timothy (2 Tim. 1:7). What should we do about it?

# 8 A call to separation

(9:1-15)

In our last chapter we commented on how few were the exiles who accompanied Ezra back to Jerusalem, and we gave as one reason for this the fact that many Jews had become absorbed into the worldly, glittering life of Babylon, and had lost the vision of themselves as God's chosen people.

**B**ut if Ezra expected things to be very different among the Jews now that he was back in the homeland, then he was to be bitterly disappointed. For they, too, like their fellow-Jews in Babylon, had lost their sense of divine calling and had become absorbed, through intermarriage, into the life of the pagan nations around them.

When these things were done, the leaders came to me, saying, "The people of Israel and the priests and the Levites have not separated themselves from the peoples of the lands ... For they have taken some of their daughters as wives for

themselves and their sons, so that the holy seed is mixed with the peoples of those lands. Indeed, the hand of the leaders and rulers has been foremost in this trespass"
(9:1-2).

## A spiritual, not racial, problem

Ezra was devastated when he was told of the people's unfaithfulness, especially to learn that the priests and Levites had led the way in this act of spiritual betrayal. We are back here to the matter of failure in leadership, which we dealt with in our last chapter. Ezra was beside himself with grief: 'So when I heard this thing, I tore my garment and my robe, and plucked out some of the hair of my head and beard, and sat down astonished' (9:3).

He could hardly believe what he was hearing. But I can imagine there might be some who would describe his response in tearing his robe and plucking hair from his head and beard as being 'a bit over the top'. 'Why this overreaction?' they would ask. But that is to totally misunderstand the nature and gravity of the offence. In the first place, Ezra was not upset because Jews had married those of another nation. The situation had nothing whatever to do with racial prejudice, since there is nothing in Scripture which prevented God's people from marrying those of another race or nation, provided they were prepared to worship the true and living God.

Indeed, there are several instances of such marriages recorded in Scripture. We read in Numbers: 'Then Miriam and Aaron spoke against Moses because of the Ethiopian woman whom he had married' (Num. 12:1). But the Scriptures themselves make no comment on this, since it would only have been wrong if the Ethiopian woman had continued to worship her own national gods. But clearly she was one with Moses in the worship of the Lord God of Israel, since as God's spokesman Moses himself had said, 'When the LORD your God brings you into the land which you go to possess, and has cast out many nations before you … seven nations greater and mightier than you … you shall make no covenant with them nor show mercy to them. Nor shall you make marriages with them. You shall not give your daughter to their son, nor take their daughter for your son' (Deut. 7:1-3).

Another example of interracial marriage was that of Boaz and Ruth. He was a godly Jew and she was a Moabitess. But prior to the marriage taking place, Ruth had identified herself positively with God's people. Her testimony of faith made to Naomi her mother-in-law is deeply moving:

> Entreat me not to leave you,
> Or to turn back from following after you;
> For wherever you go, I will go;
> And wherever you lodge, I will lodge;
> Your people shall be my people,
> And your God, my God.
> Where you die, I will die,
> And there will I be buried.
> The LORD do so to me, and more also,
> If anything but death parts you and me
> (Ruth 1:16-17).

What is of particular interest is the fact that, through her marriage to Boaz and the birth of her son Obed, Ruth the Moabitess would become an ancestress of the Messiah, the

Lord Jesus Christ. Matthew records that detail in his genealogy of Jesus (Matt. 1:5).

## Separation

The reason Ezra was so upset about the foreign marriages was because such pagan alliances meant that the people had broken faith with their covenant God, the God who had called them out from among all the nations of the earth to be his own special people, and to be a regenerating element in the world. Had these marriages with idolatrous wives been allowed to continue unchecked, the Jews would eventually have become absorbed in the surrounding mass of paganism, and God's purpose would have been frustrated. Israel was meant to be a separated people. Ezra was right therefore to react in the way he did.

There is surely a lesson in all this for God's people in the church today. For the same call to a life of separation applies to us as it did to the people of Ezra's time. Writing to the Corinthian Christians, Paul says, 'do not be unequally yoked together with unbelievers. For what fellowship has righteousness with

> Ezra was so upset about the foreign marriages because such pagan alliances meant that the people had broken faith with their covenant God, the God who had called them out from among all the nations of the earth to be his own special people, and to be a regenerating element in the world.

lawlessness? And what communion has light with darkness? And what accord has Christ with Belial? Or what part has a believer with an unbeliever?' (2 Cor. 6:14-15).

Of course, we know that the kind of separation the New Testament talks about is of a spiritual and not a physical nature. Nowhere does the gospel urge upon us the monastic principle of turning our backs upon the world in order to live our Christian lives in isolation. In fact, in his high priestly prayer (John 17) the Lord Jesus, in praying for his disciples, distinctly says: 'I do not pray that you should take them out of the world, but that you should keep them from the evil one' (v. 15).

And when John wrote in his letter, 'Do not love the world or the things in the world. If anyone loves the world, the love of the father is not in him' (1 John 2:15), he was not thinking of the created world as such, or even the people in the world. He was thinking of human society organized without reference to God, and based upon sinful principles and motivated by false values. That is the world from which Christians are to be separate, even though we have to work and live in it every day. We are to be in the world, but not part of it.

And when we reflect upon it, we can see the sense of that. For what can we believers in Christ have in common with a world like ours, which makes a god of its pleasures, is dominated by the senses, pays no regard to the commands and judgements of God, and acts in an arrogant manner that denies even the existence of God? To be overfamiliar with this world will mean that the corrosive of worldliness will quickly eat away the marks of God's grace in our lives.

Yet the sad truth is that we see this worldly spirit and attitude creeping more and more into the church today, and there are those Christians, even pastors, who can, by some kind of mental gymnastics, convince themselves that worldliness is perfectly compatible with their spiritual calling. Their argument is that, if we are to attract people to church services, and to an acceptance of the Christian message, then we must get alongside them and show that we are not so very different after all. But the whole emphasis of the gospel, surely, is to show the world that we *are different, very different* from the attitudes and opinions prevailing in society. Granted, we may find it very difficult to live this separated life because there is a natural tendency in all of us to dislike being different from the accepted norms (in any case it is always easier to conform); but the teaching of Scripture is quite clear: 'And do not be conformed to this world, but be transformed by the renewing of your mind, that you may prove what is that good and acceptable and perfect will of God' (Rom. 12:2).

May God give us a healthy detestation of that flabby, laid-back kind of Christianity that carries with it little conviction, and wants to embrace everybody. Let us instead be strong and faithful to biblical principles, whatever the cost, for there is no doubt that the worldly, lukewarm, ineffective Christian is the bane of the modern church.

## The exceeding sinfulness of sin

Ezra's strong reaction to the people's sin, seen in the tearing of his garments and the plucking of hair from his head and beard, appears to have had an immediate effect upon many of the Israelites. 'Then everyone who trembled at the words of the God of Israel assembled to me, because of the transgression of those who had been carried away captive, and I sat astonished until the evening sacrifice' (9:4).

Why did those who assembled around Ezra tremble? Was it because his dramatic reaction in tearing his clothes and plucking hair from his head and beard made them realize the seriousness of the people's sin, and how they had transgressed God's law? Were they perhaps afraid that God would be angry and bring judgement upon the nation? For what is sin? According to John it is 'the transgression of the law' (1 John 3:4 AV), a rebellion against God's revealed will. Our forefathers took such transgression seriously and used to speak of 'the exceeding sinfulness of sin', an expression we hear little of today—even in Christian circles.

Certainly our modern world is not worried about its sins; instead—under the influence of popular psychology—people are told not to burden themselves with any sense of guilt for their wrongdoing since that will only add to their stress and their sense of low self-esteem. In other words, we are fast becoming a no-fault, no-blame society in which self-analysis is confused with self-excuse.

But all this is far removed from the Bible's view of sin and guilt; it clearly states, 'All have sinned and fall short of the glory of God' (Rom. 3:23). We are all to blame, therefore, in the sense that we are all guilty before a holy God. We need, then, to have a profound hatred of sin and to see it for what it really is—a radical alienation from God and his truth—and we should be as distressed as Ezra was when we ourselves are guilty of it, and when we see the violence and corruption that the sinful heart of man inflicts upon our world.

## Intercessory prayer

The remainder of this chapter from verse 5 is concerned with Ezra's prayer of intercession on behalf of the people: 'At the evening sacrifice I arose from my fasting; and having torn my garment and my robe, I fell on my knees and spread out my hands to the LORD my God' (9:5).

The prayer that follows is deeply moving and highly instructive, as we shall see shortly. But first we must say something about intercessory prayer for others, which is a very powerful ministry and one which the Bible encourages us to engage in. Samuel was so aware of the importance of it and the need to pray for his people that he regarded it as a sin not to do so: 'Moreover, as for me, far be it from me that I should sin against the LORD in ceasing to pray for you' (1 Sam. 12:23). And the intercession of Moses on behalf of the people following the incident of the golden calf is one of the most passionate pleas recorded in the Scriptures: 'Yet now, if you will forgive their sin—but if not, I pray, blot me out of your book which you have written' (Exod. 32:32). We might mention Abraham's prayer for the righteous people in Sodom (Gen. 18:16-33), and the prayer of the church when Peter was in prison (Acts 12:5).

Intercessory prayer, therefore, is a powerful weapon in the armoury of God's people, especially when it is wielded collectively by a group of Christians who between them can harness all the powers of heaven. But not only is intercessory prayer a powerful weapon, it is also a secret weapon. We may have those people, perhaps in our family, whom we long to see coming to faith in Christ. But they make it perfectly clear that they have no wish to talk about it, and that can make us feel frustrated and helpless. But what they cannot do is stop us praying for them, and they need not even know that we are doing so. It is our secret weapon.

## Ezra's prayer

When we come to the prayer itself we notice, first of all, Ezra's approach to God. He was very humble and contrite: 'And I said: "O my God, I am too ashamed and humiliated to lift up my face to you, my God; for our iniquities have risen higher than our heads, and our guilt has grown up to the heavens" ' (9:6).

There is a balance to be struck in the matter of prayer, intercessory or otherwise. On the one hand, the Scriptures tell us that we are to be bold and confident in coming to God: 'Therefore, brethren, having boldness to enter the Holiest by the blood of Jesus, by a new and living way which he consecrated for us, through the veil, that is, his flesh' (Heb. 10:19-20). But while we can be bold and confident, we must never forget that it is the eternal God we are speaking to. He is the Creator, and we are the creatures; he is holy, we are unworthy; he is immortal and we are mortal. Being intimate in prayer with God as a loving heavenly Father is not the same thing as being 'familiar' with God.

Whenever we approach God in prayer, therefore, it ought to be, as the writer to the Hebrews goes on to say later, 'with reverence and godly fear. For our God is a consuming fire' (Heb. 12:28-29).

## Personal responsibility

There are several points of emphasis worth noting in the content of Ezra's prayer. In the first place, he stresses the doctrine of personal responsibility in regard to sin. 'Our iniquities have risen higher than our heads, and our guilt has grown up to the heavens. Since the days of our fathers to this day we have been very guilty, and for our iniquities we, our kings, and our priests have been delivered into the hand of the kings of the lands, to the sword, to captivity, to plunder, and to humiliation, as it is this day' (9:6-7).

He does not lay the blame on the heathen for mixing with the people of God, but he *does* blame the people of God for mixing with the heathen. It was they who had the light and knowledge of God's truth and therefore the responsibility for living up to that truth fell squarely on their shoulders.

The doctrine of personal responsibility is taught very clearly in the Scriptures. In the account of the Fall in Genesis 3, Adam and Eve were free agents in choosing between God's command and Satan's lie and therefore they were personally responsible for the judgement God brought upon them. Ezekiel knew people who blamed others for their sins, quoting the proverb, 'The fathers have eaten sour grapes, and the children's teeth are set on edge'. But he refuted that by saying, 'the soul who sins shall die' (Ezek. 18:2, 4). And the Lord Jesus said, 'For everyone to whom much is given, from him much will be required' (Luke 12:48).

From these and similar passages we learn that every person is responsible for his or her own behaviour before God. We cannot go making excuses, or putting the blame on others, as happened at the Fall when Adam blamed the woman and the woman blamed the serpent. This shifting of responsibility is characteristic of today's society. Man sees himself as the victim of heredity and environment, and uses that as an excuse for his behaviour. He even blames God when it suits his argument. He looks at the suffering in the world and says, in effect: 'Why does not God do something about it? It's his fault, anyway, for not making the world a better place than it is.' But God did make it better than it is. 'God saw everything that he had made, and indeed it was very good' (Gen. 1:31). It was man himself who messed things up through sin and disobedience, but he refuses to accept responsibility for that.

> Man sees himself as the victim of heredity and environment, and uses that as an excuse for his behaviour. He even blames God when it suits his argument.

Ezra was absolutely right to place the responsibility for the sin that had been committed on the shoulders of God's own people. 'Here we are before you, in our guilt, though no one can stand before you because of this!' (9:15).

## Mercy and grace

The second emphasis is the reminder that, in spite of our sin and guilt, and the failure to honour God, he is merciful and gracious to his people. 'And now for a little while grace has been shown from the LORD our God, to leave us a remnant to escape, and to give us a peg in his holy place, that our God may enlighten our eyes and give us a measure of revival in our bondage. For we were slaves. Yet our God did not forsake us in our bondage; but he extended mercy to us in the sight of the kings of Persia, to revive us, to repair the house of our God, to rebuild its ruins, and to give us a wall in Judah and Jerusalem' (9:8-9).

Ezra is well aware that, were it not for God's mercy and grace, they would not be back in the holy land, nor would the temple have been rebuilt. And he is telling God that in the present crisis it is his grace alone they can look to, in order for the spiritual health of the nation to be revived again. And how right he is. For where would any of us be without God's grace? It was through grace that we were saved, and it is by God's grace that we have been kept in the Christian way. For if we are perfectly honest, we have to confess that we are often poor material for God to have to work with in the modern world.

The meaning of the word grace in the context of Scripture is the *free unmerited love of God*. And when I read about the lives of men like Abraham, Jacob, Moses, David and Jonah, I am greatly encouraged that, although they too were weak and sinful and acted at times in a shameful and despicable manner, God did not reject them, but by grace he forgave their sins and even continued to use them in his service.

For the Christian believer, each day brings its own challenges to our faith, but there is always a fresh supply of God's grace to see us through. When faith is weak, grace strengthens us; when we are discouraged and depressed, grace can lift us up; when our hearts grow cold, grace warms them with the fire of God's love.

Amazing grace! How sweet the sound,
That saved a wretch like me!
I once was lost, but now am found;
Was blind, but now I see.

Through many dangers, toils and snares
I have already come;
'Tis grace has brought me safe thus far,
And grace will lead me home.[7]

## Eyes wide open

Another matter that burdened Ezra's heart was the sheer wilfulness of the people in their sin of entering into marriages with those from the surrounding pagan nations. It was not the sin of ignorance, but what they did, they did with their eyes wide open: 'And now, O our God, what shall we say after this? For we have forsaken your commandments, which you commanded by your servants the prophets, saying, "The land which you are entering to possess is an unclean land, with the uncleanness of the peoples of the lands, with their abominations which have filled it from one end to another with their impurity. Now therefore, do not give your daughters as wives for their sons, nor take their daughters to your sons; and never seek their peace or prosperity, that you may be strong and eat the good of the land, and leave it as an inheritance to your children forever" ' (9:10-12).

Clearly it grieved Ezra that the people were guilty of sinning against the light, and that is what made it so terrible in God's sight. If we are to learn anything from this it is that, even as God's people, the principle of sin is not entirely eradicated in our lives as long as we are living in this sinful and fallen world. We all experience time after time those occasions when the old sinful nature pushes itself up to the surface of our lives, causing us to give way to temptation and to act in a way totally contrary to the gospel. In short, we sin with our eyes wide open.

This relentless persistence of the principle of evil in our lives is related to the practical side of sanctification, the desire for holiness. The classic passage in Scripture dealing with this is in Romans 7: 'For the good that I will to do, I do not do; but the evil I will not to do, that I practise... For I delight in the law of God according to the inward man. But I see another law in my members, warring against the law of my mind, and bringing me into captivity to the law of sin which is in my members. O wretched man that I am! Who will deliver me from this body of death? I thank God— through Jesus Christ our Lord! So then, with the mind I myself serve the law of God, but with the flesh the law of sin' (Rom. 7:19-25).

Paul is surely telling us two things. First, this relentless struggle between the desire to live a holy life and the intrusion of our old sinful nature is not a hopeless battle, for 'through Jesus Christ our Lord' there is power to help us live triumphantly. And second, a time will come when God will deliver us finally from this terrible conflict, for in heaven sin will be left behind for ever.

## FOR FURTHER STUDY

1. Separation of God's people from the prevailing culture occurs in many forms in the Bible. Read Genesis 46:31-34 to see Joseph's attempt to keep his brothers separate from Egyptian culture; and Genesis 24 for the instruction by Abraham to get a wife for Isaac from among his own people.

2. In the New Testament, this separation is called sanctification, or holiness of life. Read Colossians 3:1-10. What does this passage tell us we should do?

3. The question of race is in the forefront of thinking today. Read Genesis 11:1-9 and Acts 17:24-29; what do we learn here of God's plans for the nations?

## TO THINK ABOUT AND DISCUSS

1. Why is 'separation from the world' important for Christians? What is meant by it? What is not meant? What are the implications for our Christian walk and witness if we fail to be separate?

2. Is prayer something that can be taught? If so, who should teach it in the church? What else can we do to improve our praying?

3. Discuss the different aspects of prayer: intercession, thanksgiving, petition, etc. How can a better understanding of these different aspects improve our prayer meetings and make them a greater blessing?

4. In what ways does society today minimize personal responsibility? How has this affected the lives of Christians?

5. What is meant by the following: God's common grace, saving grace, and keeping grace? What evidence of these have you seen in your own life?

# 9 Repentance and reformation

(10:1-44)

In this final chapter we see Ezra's prayer being remarkably answered in the response of the people.

His sense of burden and distress over the people's sin communicated itself to them, and a large crowd of weeping men, women and children gathered around him to make their feelings known, and to enquire as to what would happen next.

## A repentant people

Now while Ezra was praying, and while he was confessing, weeping, and bowing down before the house of God, a very large assembly of men, women, and children gathered to him from Israel; for the people wept very bitterly. And Shechaniah the son of Jehiel, one of the sons of Elam, spoke up and said to Ezra, "We have trespassed against our God, and have taken pagan wives from the peoples of the land; yet now there is hope in Israel in spite of this. Now therefore, let us make a covenant with our God to put away all these wives and those who have been born to them, according to the advice of my master and of those who tremble at the commandment of our God; and let it be done according to the law. Arise, for this matter is your responsibility. We also are with you. Be of good courage, and do it"

(10:1-4).

Clearly, what we have here is a picture of a people exhibiting all the characteristics of true repentance. I say 'true', because there is such a thing as false repentance, or repentance that is superficial and defective in God's sight. So what are the ingredients of true biblical repentance? Well, let us look at this question, first from the negative aspect, and then from the positive.

### Repentance is not just being sorry

People can sometimes think they have repented when in fact they have not actually done so. They feel sorry for what they have said or done, and think that is sufficient. But it is not. We can feel sorry and ashamed because of something we have said or done, but without any reference to God whatsoever. True biblical repentance, on the other hand, will always involve the recognition that our sin is sin against the holiness of God, and that is what makes it so serious. David says in his penitential psalm, 'Against you, you only, have I sinned, and done this evil in your sight' (Ps. 51:4). This psalm was written in connection with his sin in committing adultery with Bathsheba and then murdering her husband Uriah (2 Sam. 11). He was recognizing that he had sinned not only against Bathsheba and Uriah, but, more importantly, against God's holiness.

Likewise, when the people gathered around Ezra, and Shechaniah made confession on their behalf, he too was aware of the fact that it was against the God of the covenant they had sinned. 'And Shechaniah the son of Jehiel, one of the sons of Elam, spoke up and said to Ezra, "We have trespassed against our God, and have taken pagan wives from the peoples of the land"' (10:2).

He was aware of the enormity of what they had done as God's covenant people, and that sin is not something we should simply feel sorry for—as though it is a mere mishap, or mistake, or misdemeanour—but that it is, as we said earlier, a radical alienation from God and a contempt for his holiness.

### Repentance is not remorse

We must not confuse repentance with remorse, because remorse is negative whereas repentance is positive. What do I mean? Well, look at it like this. Judas was filled with deep and profound remorse after he had betrayed the Lord Jesus, and Matthew says that he 'went and hanged himself' (Matt. 27:5). That was a terrible price to pay for his sin. But Satan is a hard taskmaster, and Judas had deliberately sold himself to Satan. Remorse is negative in the sense that it expresses total despair and hopelessness, and engenders self-revulsion because there is no hope of forgiveness. For Judas, his self-revulsion was so intolerable that he could not live with it.

True repentance, on the other hand, is positive because it opens up the way to forgiveness, peace and reconciliation. In making confession for the people, Shechaniah was able to say, 'Yet now there is hope in Israel in spite of this' (10:2). True repentance brings not despair but hope, not emptiness but joy, not condemnation but forgiveness. If the prodigal in our Lord's parable (Luke 15) had felt only remorse for his foolish behaviour he might have said: 'Well, I've got myself into this hole and there is no way my father is going to get me out of it if I go back home, so I might as well put an end to it now.' Instead, he repented, and returned home to forgiveness and reconciliation with his father.

When we turn to the positive side of repentance we find that the following ingredients will always be present:

**DEEP CONTRITION** *True repentance will always have at its centre a sense of brokenness before God because we know that we have grieved and wounded his Spirit.* The psalmist says:

The sacrifices of God are a broken spirit,

A broken and a contrite heart—

These, O God, you will not despise

(Ps. 51:17).

When the people gathered around Ezra, we can see that they were truly contrite because we are told 'the people wept very bitterly' (10:1). Do we ever weep over our sins? Peter sinned badly when he denied the Lord three times, but he also repented in deep sorrow and tears. 'And the Lord turned and looked at Peter. Then Peter remembered the word of the Lord, how he had said to him, "Before the rooster crows, you will deny me three times." So Peter went out and wept bitterly' (Luke 22:61-62). And the picture Jeremiah gives of true repentance is that of the plough breaking up the hard soil: 'Break up your fallow ground, and do not sow among thorns' (Jer. 4:3). Just as the hard ground remains full of thorns until the plough has bitten deeply into it, so the hard heart needs to be broken with the tears of contrition so that the seed of forgiveness might enter. 'For godly sorrow produces repentance leading to salvation, not to be regretted' (2 Cor. 7:10).

**CHANGE OF DIRECTION** *True repentance will always involve a change of mind and attitude, and a change in the direction of one's life and behaviour. This is necessary as an evidence that the repentance is genuine.* In his preaching, John the Baptist exhorted the people, 'Therefore bear fruits worthy of repentance' (Matt. 3:8). And when Shechaniah confessed the sin of the people he said to Ezra, 'Now therefore, let us make a covenant with our God to put away all these wives and those who have been born to them, according to the advice of my master and of those who tremble at the commandment of our God; and let it be done according to the law. Arise, for this matter is your responsibility. We also are with you. Be of good courage, and do it' (10:3-4).

Shechaniah, it would seem, was determined to show God that the people would change both their attitude and behaviour as an evidence that their repentance was real. And God wants that change of direction from us when we repent of wrongdoing. It is no use having good intentions and not doing anything about it.

**A DAILY EXERCISE** *The final thought on repentance is that the Christian believer will practise it daily, since not a day passes without us falling into some sin or other. Ours is a constant battle with the world, the flesh and the devil, and at some point during the course of a day we are sure to require forgiveness for some weakness or failure.* The old saints of years ago used to say, 'Keep short accounts with God.' They meant quite simply that the moment we fall into sin we should repent of it. Otherwise, if it is left, it will get buried and forgotten. But God does not forget, and as long as it remains unrepented of, it will cast a shadow over the life of our soul.

God in his graciousness and mercy has promised to forgive us. 'If we confess our sins, he is faithful and just to forgive us our sins and to cleanse us from all unrighteousness' (1 John 1:9).

## God's man for the hour

Following the people's confession and repentance of their sin, we come, in the second part of this chapter, to the reformation that followed. Shechaniah, the people's spokesman, had made a very stirring speech in which he suggested that his proposal, that they put away their pagan wives and enter into a covenant with God, should be put into operation immediately. And he was in no doubt that the man to undertake this reformation of the nation's spiritual life was Ezra. He was uniquely qualified to do this as a scribe and teacher of God's Word, and as the governor of Judah. Shechaniah also assured him that he would have the support of the people: 'Arise, for this matter is your responsibility. We also are with you. Be of good courage, and do it' (10:4).

Ezra was God's man for the hour. In every great movement of the Spirit of God, both in Scripture and in the church's history, God has always raised up men of his own choosing; men who have taken his word seriously and have shown themselves willing to take on the responsibilities of leadership with all that that entails. Sometimes it calls for great courage in going against the tide of popular opinion, as in the case of Noah: 'By faith Noah, being divinely warned of things not yet seen, moved with godly fear, prepared an ark for the saving of his household, by which he condemned the world and became heir of the righteousness which is according to faith' (Heb. 11:7).

The expression 'godly fear' tells us that Noah took God and his Word seriously. The people of his day certainly did not take the warning of a flood seriously, and Noah showed great courage in continuing to build his ark when the people must have laughed at him and treated him as a madman. But he did not fear men, because he feared God more. Abraham, Joseph, Moses, Elijah, Peter and Paul were all men of that spiritual calibre; chosen of God to meet the crisis of the day in which they lived.

It may be that we have been called of God, to a much lesser degree, to take on the leadership role. If so we shall need to be men of the same spiritual integrity, and to show the same courage in standing alone for God if the occasion demands it. One thing we can be certain of is this: God will give us the same grace for the task in hand as he gave to Ezra and the others we have mentioned.

## Doing the difficult thing

Sometimes in the service of God, particularly in the leadership role, God asks us to do the hard and difficult thing, which can cause distress both to ourselves and to others. This was certainly true in Ezra's case, The reformation he was about to embark on involved breaking up marriages and families, with all the unhappiness and distress that that was bound to bring. But he did not shirk this responsibility. 'Then Ezra arose, and made the leaders of the priests, the Levites, and all Israel swear an oath that they would do according to this word. So they swore an oath' (10:5).

First, Ezra wanted to make certain that the other leaders were with him in carrying out this distasteful and difficult undertaking. But then he went further, and issued a proclamation for all the people to gather in the square in front of the house of God. 'So all the men of Judah and Benjamin gathered at Jerusalem within three days. It was the ninth month, on the twentieth of the month; and all the people sat in the open square of the house of God, trembling because of this matter and because of heavy rain' (10:9).

What a picture of absolute misery! The ninth month (Chislev) is our December and was the beginning of the rainy season. The people are cold, wet and trembling because of the distress their sin and disobedience had brought upon them. The scene made it all the harder for Ezra to do what he had to do. But he still did it! His message to the people was short and decisive: 'Then Ezra the priest stood up and said to them, "You have transgressed and have taken pagan wives, adding to the guilt of Israel. Now therefore, make confession to the LORD God of your fathers, and do his will; separate yourselves from the peoples of the land, and from the pagan wives." Then all the assembly answered and said with a loud voice, "Yes! As you have said, so we must do" ' (10:10-12).

Yes, in the service of God we are sometimes faced with having to do the hard and difficult thing which we would much rather avoid. In the pastoral ministry, it is difficult to have to reprimand a church member for some indiscretion, or to refuse to marry a couple because they are not 'equally yoked', or to request the resignation of a member from a position because he or she is failing to fulfil it competently. But the faithful pastor will not avoid acting in these situations, for the honour of God is involved.

In the Bible, the classic example of all this is the ministry of the prophet Hosea. To illustrate the unfaithfulness of Israel, God commanded him to marry an adulterous wife, and two of her children were born outside of the marriage (Hosea 1:2-8). That was really difficult, but Hosea was obedient. Jonah, on the other hand, responded with disobedience when God commanded him to preach his word to the Gentile Ninevites—he ran away from the difficult task. Next time we are faced with doing the difficult thing for God, let us pray for the courage to face up to it, and not run away.

## The task undertaken

Because it was the beginning of the rainy season, and because of the intricacies associated with divorce proceedings, it was decided to set up a commission to investigate each of the mixed marriages. ' "But there are many people; it is the season for heavy rain, and we are not able to stand outside. Nor is this the work of one or two days, for there are many of us who have transgressed in this matter. Please, let the leaders of our entire assembly stand, and let all those in our cities who have taken pagan wives come at appointed times, together with the elders and judges of their cities, until the fierce wrath of our God is turned away from us in this matter." Only Jonathan the son of Asahel and Jahaziah the son of Tikvah opposed this, and Meshullam and Shabbethai the Levite gave them support' (10:13-15).

So it was not all plain sailing. There was a small minority against the whole procedure. We are bound to ask, why? Was it because they considered the remedy too costly? It meant the break-up of their homes and marriages, and separation from their children. We can partly sympathize with them, for the outlook was positively heart-breaking. But there are two things to be kept in mind.

If the opposers were themselves guilty of mixed marriages, then it was their own sin and disobedience that led to the heartbreak they were experiencing. Rejection of God always leads ultimately to misery and suffering. Modern man, in his pride and intellectual arrogance, believes he can go his own way independently of God his Creator. But we have only to look at our world to see the miserable mess this boastful, progressive (so-called) spirit has made of it.

Then again, if, as we have suggested, the opposers considered the price of being faithful to God's Word to be too costly, then that also carries a lesson. We would be foolish to expect there to be no cost involved in serving God, or that being a Christian need not make any difference to our way of life. When Scott of the Antarctic was building up his team, he was inundated by enthusiasts offering their services. But he had to weed out the realists from the romantics, and warned: 'Are you ready to meet the snow, the ice and the bitter winds; insufficient food, exhaustion, weariness, and the boredom of it all?'

If that was true of following Scott to the Antarctic, how much more true is it when it comes to following the Lord

Jesus in the way of the cross? There must be cost. Jesus himself said so. 'Blessed are you when they revile and persecute you, and say all kinds of evil against you falsely for my sake.' But we are not to be depressed by that, because he then said, 'Rejoice and be exceedingly glad, for great is your reward in heaven' (Matt. 5:11-12). Whatever the cost in following Christ, it is all worth it in the end.

## A satisfactory ending

The commission got under way and, over the next three months, carried out its work painfully and with great thoroughness. 'Ezra the priest, with certain heads of the fathers' households, were set apart by the fathers' households, each of them by name; and they sat down on the first day of the tenth month to examine the matter. By the first day of the first month they finished questioning all the men who had taken pagan wives' (10:16-17).

It had been a momentous experience for Israel, with much prayer, and tears, and a lot of heartbreak. But now the nation was restored, cleansed and forgiven, and back in its covenant relationship with God. For the child of God, there is always a way back.

## Reformation or revival?

Before leaving this fascinating piece of biblical history there is one further issue to be considered. Was what happened under the leadership of Ezra a reformation or a revival? The two movements are entirely different. While I believe there were revivals in the Old Testament, I do not think we can use that term to describe what took place in Ezra's time. Revival comes from above, reformation comes from below. In revival, the supernatural element is uppermost in a mighty outpouring of the Spirit of God upon his people, the church. In reformation the human element is largely at work in taking the initiative to plan and organize in order to bring about change for the better.

In our study of Ezra it appears to me that what we have is a reformation of God's people in order to bring them back into conformity with God's will and purpose. The Holy Spirit was clearly at work in the hearts of the people, but not in the sense in which we normally associate the Holy Spirit in revival, when there is a supernatural spiritual awakening which is sudden and unplanned.

When we consider what happened at the Reformation in the sixteenth century under Martin Luther we see the difference. He initiated a movement to reform the structure of the church, and to correct spiritual abuses by sound biblical teaching. That is what we have in Ezra. The leaders initiated the reformation when they came to Ezra and informed him of the abuse of mixed marriages among God's people, the church: 'The leaders came to me, saying, "The people of Israel and the priests and the Levites have not separated themselves from the peoples of the lands, with respect to the abominations of the Canaanites..." ' (9:1).

Ezra—as a scribe and teacher of God's Word in the Law—could see that the people needed to be taught afresh the doctrine of separation as contained in the Law. He then undertook to put the necessary reforms into operation by organizing a proclamation, and setting up a commission of elders and judges from each town and city to investigate the mixed marriages. The whole procedure covered a period of three months. It was a restructuring process and was done with great thoroughness and much prayer.

So what relevance does this have for us in the church today? It tells us that, whereas we long for revival in the church but cannot make it happen, we can nevertheless bring about a reformation where it is needed. Pastors, deacons and members can reform the structures of their local church so as to make its witness more effective in the community. Indeed, this is happening all the time in different parts of the UK. Churches are reforming the structures of their services, the times of worship, the forms of outreach, and the work among young people. All this calls for planning and organization, and, above all, much prayer and the desire to do everything in conformity to God's will, based on sound biblical teaching. It must never be reformation and change for its own sake.

Reformation of this kind is not only desirable in many churches, but is vitally necessary if the gospel is to meet the challenges of today, and the church is to remain relevant in the age in which God has set us.

Reformation may also be needed not only in the church but also in our personal lives. We all need, from time to time, to take a good hard look at the structure of our own lifestyles, and ask ourselves if they need reforming in line with what God asks of us. What of our prayer life, our faithfulness at the worship services, our input into the local church, our financial contribution to God's work, our missionary support, etc.? These are all aspects that may need reforming in order to give a sharper edge to our Christian experience and witness.

Revival is what we desperately need today. No Christian believer can seriously doubt that. But since that is entirely in God's realm and sovereignty, we can in the meantime get on with the work of reformation when needed, whether in the church or in our personal life.

## The conclusion

So we come to the end of our exposition of the book of Ezra. But the history of the return of God's people from exile does not end at this point. It continues in the book of Nehemiah. But Ezra himself is no longer the main figure. His work of reformation is done, and although he continues to serve God's people his role will be subordinate to that of Nehemiah, the new civil governor of Judah. As a scribe and teacher of God's law, Ezra had instructed the people in the way of holiness, and had called them back to obedience within God's covenant. Henceforth he would be perfectly prepared to adopt a subordinate role, and that carries a lesson for all Christian leaders.

First, are we prepared to recognize when the work God has called us to do is done? And are we prepared to let go when our usefulness is passed and the work itself begins to suffer as a result? Second, are we prepared when our own leadership role comes to an end, to accept—if necessary—a subordinate role, as Ezra did under Nehemiah?

For further study ▶

1. To learn more about God choosing special people for particular tasks, read Jeremiah 1:4-10, Exodus 3-4, and Galatians 1:11-17.

2. Read Luke 22:54-62, John 21:15-17, and Matthew 27:1-5. What, in the light of these passages, is the difference between true repentance and remorse?

3. 'God has special people for special tasks', e.g. Ezra. What other examples can you think of in the Bible, and what was the purpose for which God raised each one up?

## TO THINK ABOUT AND DISCUSS

1. What do you think happened under Ezra: reformation or revival? Can reformation lead to revival, and revival lead to reformation?

2. In our churches, why is it difficult for people sometimes to let go of positions they have held when they should withdraw? How can we encourage them to be willing to let others take on their role? Are there any practical things we could do to help this process?

3. Having read through this book, what do you consider to be the most important lessons or principles that you have learned? How do you think these may transform your life and the lives of others?

# Endnotes

1 Thomas O. Chisholm, *Great is Thy faithfulness.*

2 C. S. Lewis, *Screwtape Letters—Screwtape proposes a toast*, Fontana, 1965.

3 Iain H. Murray, *The Unresolved Controversy: unity with non-evangelicals*, Banner of Truth, 2001, p. 27.

4 Frances Ridley Havergal, *Take my life.*

5 James Philip, *A Time to Build*, Didasko Press, 1977, p. 65.

6 Henry Emerson Fosdick, *God of grace and God of glory.*

7 John Newton, *Amazing grace!*

 The Opening up series

Further titles in preparartion

This fine series is aimed at the 'average person in the church' and combines brevity, accuracy and readability with an attractive page layout. Thought-provoking questions make the books ideal for both personal or small group use.

**'Laden with insightful quotes and penetrating practical application, Opening up Philippians is a Bible study tool which belongs on every Christian's bookshelf!'**

DR. PHIL ROBERTS, PRESIDENT, MIDWESTERN BAPTIST THEOLOGICAL SEMINARY, KANSAS CITY, M I S S O U R I

Please contact us for a free catalogue

**In the UK** ☎ 01568 613 740    **email—** sales@dayone.co.uk

**In the United States:** ☎ Toll Free:1-8-morebooks

**In Canada:** ☎ 519  763  0339 www.dayone.co.uk